P9-DHJ-874

QUESTIONS FOR GOOD GRAMMAR

1. Correct the subject-verb agreement:
   The array of educational programs benefit both the students and the company.

2. Correct the errors in capitalization, hyphenation, and apostrophe use:
   I think you can say our company is over regulated. We have sixty-six Policies for operating the elevators' safely.

3. Identify the questionable construction, and correct it:
   While away at the conference, my desk was moved into the hallway.

Answers (corrections underlined):
1. The array of educational programs benefits both the students and the company. (Subject of the sentence is array.)
2. I think you can say our company is over-regulated. We have sixty-six policies for operating the elevators safely.
3. While I was away at the conference, someone moved my desk into the hallway. (A dangling participle: Your desk was not away at the conference, you were.)

Also by Dianna Booher:

COPING: When Your Family Falls Apart

THE LAST CARESS

RAPE: What Would You Do If...?

MAKING FRIENDS WITH YOURSELF AND OTHER
 STRANGERS

HELP! WE'RE MOVING

WOULD YOU PUT THAT IN WRITING? How to
 Write Your Way to Success in Business

GETTING ALONG WITH PEOPLE WHO DON'T
 GET ALONG

SEND ME A MEMO: A Handbook of Model Memos

LOVE: First Aid for the Young

THE NEW SECRETARY: How to Handle People as
 Well as You Handle Paper

HOW TO WRITE YOUR WAY TO SUCCESS IN
 BUSINESS

GOOD GRIEF, GOOD GRAMMAR

Dianna Booher

FAWCETT CREST • NEW YORK

A Fawcett Crest Book
Published by Ballantine Books
Copyright © 1988 by Dianna Booher

All rights reserved under International and Pan-American Copyright Conventions. Published in the United States by Ballantine Books, a division of Random House, Inc., New York, and simultaneously in Canada by Random House of Canada Limited, Toronto.

No part of this book may be reproduced or utilized in any form or by any means, electronic or mechanical, including photocopying, recording or by any information storage and retrieval systems, without permission in writing from the Publisher.

Library of Congress Catalog Card Number: 87-27525

ISBN 0-449-21681-0

This edition published by arrangement with Facts On File, Inc.

Manufactured in the United States of America

First Ballantine Books Edition: July 1989

CONTENTS

Contents

Contents

A NOTE TO THE READER

If you want a "before" and "after" picture of your improvement, begin this book by turning to the Therapy section at the end of each chapter. Read the directions and try to complete each exercise; then turn to the Answers section in the back of the book and check your work.

With those "pretests" behind you, go back to Chapter 1 and slowly work your way through the explanations and examples of each chapter. When you come to the Therapy exercises, rework them with a different color ink or pencil. Check the answers in the back of the book and note your improvement as you move from chapter to chapter.

INTRODUCTION

The room looked like a funeral parlor transplanted to the tallest Skyscraper in Houston. The executives marched in one by one, eyes downcast and briefcases swishing to the tabletop with clicking sounds as locks opened.

John Clayton, program analyst knew this meeting would be the turning point. Assuming they would come to a decision today, the outcome would effect his career, his marriage, and probably determine the day of his murder.

The Senior Vice President took his seat at the end of the conference table; and the other assorted company officers followed his led, and shuffled into place. John kept his face blank as Marys airline tickets slid to the floor with a slight flutter. He nonchalantly retrieved it and tucked it back in his coat pocket. He began to wonder, why he'd only bought her ticket and not his also. Had he subconsciously already made his decision weeks ago—before the audit, before the programmers had cracked the code, and perhaps even before buying the $2 million shipment of size 10 negligees?

What do all these sex, money, and power details have to do with grammar? Absolutely nothing. But now that I have your attention, let me point out that you just read past fifteen grammatical errors in the opening scene. (See the corrected version on page 197.) If you didn't notice these errors, then you definitely need to keep reading; this book's for you. We're going to start with the basics and stay focused on the essentials.

But possibly I need to define "essentials." Some writers consider grammar-conscious bosses nitpickers. These writers fail to see the link between grammar and clarity.

For example,

> We will have markers and erasers that can be picked up with the key.

What does this sentence mean? That the reader can pick up markers, erasers, and the key at the same time? That the reader has to have the key for access to the markers and erasers?

Or take another example of an ambiguous statement that appeared in the *Houston Chronicle*:

> An off-duty postal worker armed with a pistol fatally wounded his estranged wife, a U.S. Marine sergeant, and then shot and killed himself in a federal office building in downtown Houston Thursday, police said.

How many people were killed—two or three? (Several paragraphs later in the news story, the reader learns that the wife *was* a U.S. Marine sergeant.)

Grammar is not a "minor" part of writing; proper grammar is an aid to clarity.

In addition to clarity, poor grammar affects a reader's attitude about the ideas presented in a document. Imagine yourself seated in a restaurant. The waiter comes with your order. He has dirt caked under his fingernails, his greasy hair hangs in his eyes, and stains of the day's specials decorate his shirt. Would his appearance affect your appetite? In much the same way, grammatical errors can sour your readers on the ideas you present in memos, letters, and reports.

In fact, many business writers have found the lack of a good foundation in grammar to be an embarrassment and a serious handicap. Despite software packages that check spelling and syntax, personal writing skills will never become obsolete.

When I lead writing workshops for corporate clients, out of a group of fifteen participants I'll invariably have five who ask me where they can find a good, comprehensive grammar text for the business writer. That's the "why" behind this book—help for those who missed the basics and who must be effective communicators.

Consider the first five chapters as first aid. There you'll find the basic definitions, principles, and examples that anyone must understand to be grammatically correct.

Some readers may ask, Do I need to know all the technical grammatical terms? Let me answer this way: How would you like to be the patient under anesthesia with this team of doctors?

"Do you think we ought to take out his whatchamacallit while we're in here?"

"His whatever, there next to it, seems a little inflamed, too."

"Hand me the thingamabob."

"The what?"

"Oh, you know, the dohickey. The stainless steel instrument. The thing that sounds like a thump when it hits a vein."

"This?"

"No, the sharper thing underneath it. The gizmo here doesn't look just right. You think we should remove it, too?"

Yes, you need to learn the terms given in the first few chapters. I hear people frequently comment, "I know when a sentence doesn't look right, but I don't know how to correct it." If you learn the appropriate terms and definitions, you'll be able to identify *and correct* grammatical errors.

Consider the remaining chapters, Chapters 6–12, part of your "stabilization" process; they build on the concepts explained in the first few chapters. Finally, each chapter has a Therapy section to help check your mastery of the concepts. The more exercises you work, the closer you will be to good grammatical health. For "maintenance and growth," apply the directions for the Therapy sections to one of your own documents from your job.

One more thing: This book is not exhaustive; for example, you'll notice that I've omitted the exclamation point in the punctuation chapter. My rule of thumb for keeping this book to the essentials has been to ask, "How often will the business writer need to know this?" If the answer was "once every fifth Sunday in February," then I've omitted the idea.

By the way, so that you won't go into shock when you see Chapter 12, let me explain the "why" of it. My theory is that people who are weak in grammar are primarily visual learners; instead of excelling in those skills typically termed verbal, they excel in analytical skills. They like to see things that make sense; that is, they like to have formulas and logical answers. What's surprising to many of these "visual" people is that most grammatical rules do make sense and follow logical patterns. For writers having trouble pinpointing why a sentence is awkward or correcting a sentence they recognize as wrong, diagraming becomes a real eye-opener. Writers see the structure and understand the accompanying logic.

Therefore, for you "visual" readers, I have added Chapter 12. You can study its appropriate sections chapter by chapter, or you can examine all of Chapter 12 after you've completed the rest of the book. The diagrams in Chapter 12 will cement in your mind the concepts learned throughout the book. If you want to prove to yourself that you've really become a grammar guru, after studying Chapter 12 try to diagram some of your own sentences.

With or without the diagrams, you can become grammatically healthy if you follow the therapeutic plan outlined in this book.

1

WORDS

Think of words as bricks. You pile them together to make phrases, clauses, and then sentences. We categorize all words into eight parts of speech: nouns, pronouns, verbs, adjectives, adverbs, prepositions, conjunctions, and interjections. The inability to recognize these parts of speech is as much a handicap as not knowing the value of nickels, dimes, quarters, and dollars.

NOUNS

A noun names a person, place, thing, activity, or idea. Nouns can be further divided into the categories that follow.

Common	Proper	Collective
desk	August	staff
payment	City Hall	audience
office	Lotus 1-2-3	personnel

1

eye	Phoenix, Arizona	group
women	Hortense Hoffnaggle	management
customer	Mojave Desert	team
manager	New Year's Day	committee
videotape	Lawn Avenue	jury
	Friday	

Concrete	*Abstract*
street	freedom
laundry	theory
computer	attitude
equipment	problem
money	politics
uniforms	philosophy
sugar	situation
brochure	protection
	annual report
	(no, just kidding)

Recognition of the various kinds of nouns is essential to correct capitalization and subject-verb agreement—matters we'll get into later.

VERBS

A verb is a word that shows action, being, or state of being. In other words, a verb is a word that shows what something *has, does,* or *is.*

Has	*Does*	*Is*
possess	share	seem
include	calculate	appear
contain	hide	become
retain	dazzle	smell
hold	submit	taste
own	indicate	exist
lack	teach	sound

NOTE: Don't be confused when you see these verbs in other forms and combined with helping words to make verb phrases. (You'll hear more about verb phrases in Chapter 2.)

has been sharing	should contain	perplexed
is calculated	were	were informed
does possess	taught	can promote
smelled	built	is tasting
will dazzle	had been	verify
can submit	became	conduct

When you add helping words to the main verb, the form of the main verb may change. Verbs have three principal parts:

Regular Verbs

Present	Past	Past Participle
		(formed by adding -d or -ed)
talk	talked	talked
hire	hired	hired
examine	examined	examined
identify	identified	identified
cover	covered	covered
mark	marked	marked
interview	interviewed	interviewed
call	called	called

Irregular Verbs

Present	Past	Past Participle
write	wrote	written
begin	began	begun
do	did	done
set	set	set
sit	sat	sat

am	was	been
break	broke	broken
choose	chose	chosen
teach	taught	taught
go	went	gone
drive	drove	driven
draw	drew	drawn
fly	flew	flown
sell	sold	sold
grow	grew	grown
speak	spoke	spoken

ADJECTIVES

Adjectives point out, number, and describe (or in some way tell more about) nouns or pronouns. They answer the questions: Which one? What kind? How many? How much? Words that you may have heard called "articles" (*a, an, the*) are also considered adjectives. (*A* precedes a word starting with a consonant; *an* precedes a word starting with a vowel or vowel sound: *a re*port, *a we*lcome, *an anno*tated report, *an in*volvement, *an* honor.)

The following italicized words are adjectives.

A perplexing dilemma

Several lame excuses

This condemning, flimsy, ridiculous, late report

Our future mind-boggling success

The two angry, rambling, yellowed letters

Paul's state-of-the-art computer lecture

Most adjectives have three degrees of comparison: positive, comparative, and superlative. *Positive* adjectives do not compare anything to anything. *Comparative* adjectives compare two things. *Superlative* adjectives compare three or more things.

> My report is *short*. (Does not compare)
>
> My report is *shorter* than your report. (Compares yours and mine)
>
> My report is the *shortest* report ever submitted. (Compares mine to several)

Most adjectives are compared by simply adding *-er* or *-est*.

Positive	Comparative	Superlative
quick	quicker	quickest
bright	brighter	brightest
tame	tamer	tamest
sick	sicker	sickest

Some adjectives, particularly those longer than one syllable, are compared with the help of the words *more* or *less*, *most* or *least*. (The words *more*, *most*, *less*, and *least* are adverbs—explained under the next heading.)

Positive	Comparative	Superlative
perplexing	more perplexing	most perplexing
explicit	more explicit	most explicit
enjoyable	less enjoyable	least enjoyable
complete	less complete	least complete

Some adjectives are compared in irregular forms.

Positive	Comparative	Superlative
good	better	best
ill	worse	worst

bad	worse	worst
many	more	most
much	more	most

Some adjectives are absolute and have no comparative or superlative form: *unique, round, square, perfect, empty, dead*. If something is *square*, it cannot be *more square* or *most square*. Such use shows misunderstanding about the meaning of the word.

ADVERBS

Most adverbs tell more about the main verb of a sentence. However, adverbs may also describe or explain more about an adjective, another adverb, or the sentence as a whole. Adverbs usually answer the following questions: How? Why? When? Where? To what extent? Many adverbs end in *-ly*.

firmly	sharply	not
blatantly	carefully	too
briskly	soon	there
candidly	sometimes	more
bitterly	here	now
daily	very	when
approximately	well	why
mistakenly	where	quite

Adverbs Describing or Limiting Verbs

Looking at our organizational flowchart will *always* confuse you about who *really* has the final say. (To what extent?)

He expressed his opinion *honestly* and *forthrightly*; the committee answered *deceptively* and *dogmatically*. (How did he express? How did the committee answer?)

The receptionist is resigning *immediately* after she pushes her last button. (When will she resign?)

She walked *outside* and exhaled billows of smoke. (Where did she walk?)

Adverbs Describing or Limiting Adjectives

This is a *more* appealing report than the first one; who cares if it's inaccurate? (To what extent is it appealing?)

She is a *blatantly* disgruntled boss. (To what extent is the boss disgruntled?)

He delights in presenting management with *recently* reported customer problems. (Reported when?)

Willie Sniffer is a *highly* respected individual; Sarah Snuffleboard is *clearly* upset that he is. (Respected to what extent? Upset to what extent?)

Adverbs Describing or Limiting Adverbs

He talks his way out of promotions *more* quickly than any employee I've trained. (Quick to what extent?)

I would *very* much appreciate your returning my phone call sometime this year. (Appreciate how much?)

Adverbs Describing or Limiting Sentences

Frankly, I wouldn't rubber stamp anything that committee decided.

Candidly, I haven't worked for a guy I admire less.

Adverbs, like adjectives, are compared by adding *-er* or *-est*.

Positive	Comparative	Superlative
soon	sooner	soonest
fast	faster	fastest

Some adverbs, particularly those of two or more sylla-bles, are compared by adding *more* or *less, most* or *least*. Some adverbs can be compared by either method.

Positive	Comparative	Superlative
often	oftener	oftenest
often	more often	most often
often	less often	least often

Some adverbs are compared irregularly.

Positive	Comparative	Superlative
well	better	best
badly	worse	worst

PRONOUNS

A pronoun takes the place of a noun or another pro-noun. For example, if you don't want to say *desk,* you can refer to the desk as *it.* If you don't want to say *manager,* you can refer to the manager with pronouns such as *she* or *her, he* or *him*.

Personal

I	me	my	mine
you	you	your	yours
he	him	his	his
she	her	her	hers
it	it	its	its
we	us	our	ours
they	them	their	theirs

Interrogative

what	how	why	who
whose	whom	which	

Demonstrative

this	that	these	those

Indefinite

none	most	any	all
both	neither	either	each
many	more	some	someone
nowhere	somewhere	something	somebody
anything	anybody	anywhere	nothing
nobody	no one	one	every
few	another	others	several
anyone	everyone	everybody	everything

Relative

that	why	which	whichever
what	whatever	who	whoever
whom	whomever	where	wherever

Reciprocal

each other	one another

Reflexive

yourself	myself	himself	herself
yourselves		themselves	ourselves

Possessive

his	her	hers	my
mine	your	yours	their
theirs	our	ours	its

The decision was a bad *one*.

The chairman loosened *his* tie so that *someone* would not be tempted to choke *him* with *it*.

When *you* want *something* done wrong, do *it yourself*.

PREPOSITIONS

A preposition links the noun that follows it (the object of the preposition) to another word in the sentence.

about	over	with
among	beyond	near
of	past	underneath
under	unto	within
without	against	to
during	for	across
through	in	against
above	into	since
by	down	along
beside	since	around
off	upon	onto
until	at	before
beneath	on	throughout
except	below	behind
between	after	besides
from	toward	out
up	like	inside

A few prepositions are formed with two or more words: *together with, as well as, along with, in addition to, regardless of, instead of, on account of, with respect to, ahead of, according to, by means of, in spite of, because of, down from, out of.*

The following sentences contain underlined prepositions followed by their objects. You'll hear more about these italicized prepositional phrases in Chapter 3.

prep   obj   prep   obj
In the beginning was the chairman *of the board*.

prep   obj   prep
The length *of our billing cycle* reflects the lack *of pro-*
obj   prep   obj
ductivity of our accountants.

prep   obj   prep
She sent the message *across the Atlantic Ocean by elec-*
obj
tronic means.

CONJUNCTIONS

Conjunctions connect words, phrases, and clauses. Conjunctions fall into three categories: *coordinate, subordinate,* and *correlative*. Coordinate conjunctions link things of *equal* importance. Subordinate conjunctions link a *less important* word, phrase, or idea *to a more important* word, phrase, or idea. Correlative conjunctions are used *in pairs* to connect *equal* things.

Coordinate Conjunctions

(and, but, or, for, nor, so, yet)

Tom *and* Susan need more help than they can give each other. (*Tom* and *Susan*—equal nouns)

My analysts plan *and* argue each new product idea until competitors develop it first. (Equal verbs—*plan* and *argue*)

She who pays her tuition, studies hard, *and* graduates with highest honors may find a job. (Three equal verbs in a series—*pays, studies, graduates*)

Clever advertising may sell a mediocre product, *but* a mediocre product can kill a good ad. (Two equal ideas)

Subordinate Conjunctions

(although, as, as long as, as soon as, as if, if, before, how, in order that, inasmuch as, so that, than, until, till, unless, when, whereas, whether, while, why, after, since, because)

major idea
(I can't leave) *because* she has the key to the washroom.

(*Because* introduces the lesser idea of the two.)

major idea
(She insists on a bonus) *until* I leave the project. (*Until*

introduces the minor idea.)

major idea
When all else fails, (you still have taxes.) (*When* intro-

duces the minor idea.)

major idea
(He told me his answer) *before* I asked the question.

(*Before* links the minor idea to the major idea.)

Correlative Conjunctions

(either/or, neither/nor, both/and, whether/or, whether/if, not only/but also)

Either you *or* I will have to put in a full day's work today.

This assertiveness seminar presented me with *both* the confidence *and* the stupidity to ask the boss what she thinks I'm worth.

Whether he goes *or* stays will make little difference in our reorganization plans.

INTERJECTIONS

Interjections are seldom used in business writing. They usually show strong emotion—something that most people show only after they leave a job.

Oh, you know how I feel!

Wow, no one made quota!

Well, there you have it—proof that he has been promoted two levels above his competence.

Indeed, you should consider his attitude in the performance appraisal!

We've just finished the eight parts of speech: nouns, verbs, adjectives, adverbs, pronouns, prepositions, conjunctions, interjections.

MAJOR RELAPSES

If you are going to have difficulty in recognizing parts of speech, the problem will likely be with a word that can be more than one part of speech. Part-of-speech labels change according to how a word is used in a specific sentence.

She is *working* today. (Verb)

He has prepared a *working* draft. (Adjective)

Working is the way I pass the time between weekends. (Noun)

He teaches his material very *well*. (Adverb—tells how he teaches)

He is not *well*. (Adjective—describes *he*)

We drilled a *well* with your investment; unfortunately, it was a dry hole. (Noun)

I need an extra typewriter; do you have *one?* (Pronoun—replaces the noun *typewriter*)

Yes, we have *one* typewriter in the storage closet. (Adjective—modifies *typewriter*; tells how many)

He opens the office at an *early* hour. (Adjective)

Please arrive *early* to get a seat. (Adverb)

I know it's not in your job description, but would you *hose* down the courtyard before you leave? (Verb)

Roll up the *hose* and hook it to the back of the delivery truck. (Noun)

This job is turning into work. (Adjective—describes the noun *job*)

This is turning into work. (Pronoun—replaces a noun)

I have met him *before*. (Adverb—tells when, such as *previously*)

I will meet him *before* Friday. (Preposition)

I will meet him *before* we sign the contract. (Conjunction—joins two complete ideas)

He asks for nothing *but* trouble. (Preposition—meaning *except*)

He asks for nothing, *but* I gave him plenty. (Conjunction—connects two equal ideas)

Don't be confused by words that have the same root but that have different endings and serve in diverse ways in a sentence. For example, *educate* is a verb; *education* is a noun; *educational* is an adjective.

He *educated* the department employees to his pain in having to work with them. (Verb)

He has received a real *education* since coming to work for Marlene Maddicks. (Noun)

Don't look at your sales-commission check as if it signifies failure; think of it as a tuition discount on an *educational* experience. (Adjective)

Another example: *obey, obedience, obedient*.

All accountants must *obey* the unwritten policies around here. (Verb)

Strict *obedience* is more crucial than logical reasoning and technical accuracy. (Noun)

An *obedient* accountant is an employed accountant. (Adjective)

THERAPY 1

Using the simple abbreviations here, label each word in the following sentences as to its part of speech.

noun—n	verb—v	adjective—adj
adverb—adv	conjunction—cj	interjection—ij
pronoun—pn	preposition—pp	

   pn   v   adj adj adj n pp n
1. I exhausted all my good ideas by noon.

2. The invoice was calculated incorrectly.

3. This caustic letter denounces the deficiency in brainpower around our office.

4. Regardless of the stupid ideas here, we thank you for your letter.

5. The committee and my three assistants have worked on the quarterly report diligently against false deadlines and despite other daily projects.

6. With experienced personnel, we can professionally examine all foodstuffs and, by minor repair, improve the surface imperfections before customers buy and eat them.

7. Downgrade the service and improperly install and identify each piece of equipment as we have previously authorized.

8. Jeffrey Smarts has accumulated the data for the meeting with Freda Flabbergasted.

9. This situation is a dismal one.

10. John Tactless sent them a memo about his philosophy of management and, consequently, ensured his sudden departure.

11. Either they will try my suggestion for rainy weather or someone must be all wet.

12. If you are in doubt, fire someone.

13. In our company, the difference between sales rep and director of marketing is about two good sales.

14. Our company policy mandates safety inspections every twenty years.

15. His activity report indicates everything except activity.

16. She loses enthusiasm with each new product brochure.

17. Gertrude was the role model for his book on failure.

18. To most people, paperwork ensures delay and offers self-protection.

19. Despite our installation of a voice-mail system and videoconferencing equipment, the grapevine is still our fastest mode of internal communication.

2

HOW WORDS WORK IN A SENTENCE

After you've learned to recognize the eight parts of speech, the next step toward grammatical health is learning how words function in a sentence. The major sentence functions are *subjects, verbs, direct objects, indirect objects, subject complements,* and *object complements*. The secondary sentence functions are *adjective* and *adverb* modifiers.

SUBJECTS

The *simple subject* is a noun or pronoun that tells what is being talked about in the sentence. The *complete subject* includes all the words that point out, describe, limit, or tell more about the simple subject. The simple subjects are underlined in the following sentences; the complete subjects are italicized:

19

The careless Tom Harris approved the report without reading it.

All of the tallest downtown buildings had the panes blown out.

This office with the breathtaking view is all yours.

Happy babies in nearby company-operated day-care centers put anxious parents back to work sooner than expected.

Sentences may have two or more subjects—*compound subjects*. The compound subjects are underlined in the following sentences. The complete subjects are italicized.

Both my legal assistant and my stockbroker have confided $2,000 worth of gobbledygook to me this year.

After the power failure, *Heida Heildegard, I , and the word processor with the empty screen* disappeared.

NOTE: Most subjects come at the beginning of a sentence. However, don't be confused about an inverted sentence pattern that puts the subject at the end.

Here are *the latest sales figures*.

In our analysis of the whole situation and according to the public-relations firm working on the project, there are *numerous inconsistencies in the contract*.

NOTE: Some sentences have the understood subject *you*. Such sentences are always commands.

> Please lick your wounds privately. (You lick.)
>
> Tell me what you think of the merger. (You tell.)
>
> Take your kite and fly it over someone else's sales territory. (You take.)

PREDICATES

The predicate of the sentence contains the verb and the words that tell more about or limit the verb. The *simple predicate* is the verb; the *complete predicate* is the verb and all other words that describe or limit it. In the following sentences the verbs are underlined; the complete predicates are italicized.

> My stock market analyst <u>makes</u> *predictions based on common sense and a little inside information.*

> Our banker <u>set up</u> *a loan repayment schedule with the first payment due within the hour.*

> More hidden costs of the project *<u>surface</u> daily.*

> The sample from the well site *<u>reveals</u> contaminated water, as well as an endangered species of engineer.*

If a sentence has two verbs that tell more about the subject, the verbs are called *compound predicates*. In the following sentences the complete predicates are italicized; the compound predicates (verbs) are underlined.

Ned Nuttimeyer *rejected the presidency and accepted the position of receptionist in order to meet potential customers*.

My boss *groans and curses when interrupted*.

Sheila *has read the job description and has decided to resign voluntarily*.

The dim-witted purchasing agent *decided to lease the equipment and thus changed his title to leasing agent*.

The verbs in these complete predicates are either *transitive* or *intransitive*. A transitive verb (as the arrows indicate) *transfers* action from the subject to an object that follows.

Transitive Verbs

The boss *kicked* Jack and Jill down the corporate ladder.

The controller discreetly *transferred* the funds to Switzerland.

My memos always *pose* problems rather than solutions.

The boss *skimmed* my expense report, looking for steak dinners.

He *spent* all the money budgeted for raises before getting to me.

An intransitive verb has no object. If the verb does not need an object to make a complete thought, the verb is *intransitive complete*. If the subject and verb alone do not make a complete thought, the verb is *intransitive linking*. That is, the verb links the subject with an adjective that describes it or with another word that renames the subject.

Intransitive Complete Verbs

He *walked* into the meeting with a blank stare. (The verb *walked* does not transfer any action to an object that follows it; therefore, it is *intransitive*. It is *intransitive complete* because it does not link the subject *he* to an adjective that follows or to another word that renames the subject.)

The tale about the customer who got away *grows* with each telling. (The verb *grows* does not transfer any action to an object that follows it; therefore, it is *intransitive*. It is *intransitive complete* because it does not link the subject *tale* to an adjective that follows or to another word that renames the subject.)

The meeting *was postponed*. (The verb *was postponed* does not transfer any action to an object that follows it; therefore, it is *intransitive*. It is *intransitive complete* because it does not link the subject *meeting* to an adjective that follows or to another word that renames the subject.)

The project *failed* in its early stages. (The verb *failed* does not transfer any action to an object that follows it; therefore, it is *intransitive*. It is *intransitive complete* because it does not link the subject *project* to an adjective that follows or to another word that renames the subject.)

Intransitive Linking Verbs

These verbs are like equal signs between the subjects and the nouns or objects that follow the subjects.

The client *seems* apprehensive about not having the price in writing. (*The client seems* does not make sense by itself; the verb is incomplete and merely links the adjective *apprehensive* to the subject.)

His interviewing technique *is* a stress test. (*His interviewing technique is* does not make sense by itself; the verb is incomplete and merely links the noun *test* to the subject it renames.)

Spudney Sniwtzenlender *became* president. (*Spudney Sniwtzenlender became* does not make sense by itself; the verb is incomplete and merely links the noun *president* to the subject it renames.)

The prices *are* too high. (*The prices are* does not make sense by itself; the verb is incomplete and merely links the adjective *high* to the subject.)

MODIFIERS

Modifying words always fall into one of two categories: adjectives or adverbs. *Adjective modifiers* tell more about nouns or pronouns. *Adverb modifiers* tell more about verbs, adjectives, adverbs, or the sentence as a whole. In Chapter 1, you noted adjectives and adverbs as parts of speech. Here, these sentences simply illustrate how adjectives and adverbs function in a complete sentence.

Adjective Modifiers

The July 6 Blanton report defies explanation.

The defiant chairperson slung *those heavy* chairs against *the* newly *papered* wall as she exited *our hostile* conference.

Adequate resources, *successful* formulas, and *supportive* management mean you are definitely not working for *my* company.

Adverb Modifiers

Honestly, I cannot find the *most* appropriate answer until you give me a hint about the question.

Let me know *immediately* if you can accompany me on the flight that leaves *today*.

Whatever supplies you need will be found *nowhere* on the premises.

He is a *very* patient, kind man with his employees; he shouts *only* at his wife and kids.

Apparently, his job description was part of a hoax.

Your ability to recognize adjectives and adverbs and to identify what words they tell more about (or modify) will help you use them correctly. Consider:

Bart did a *really* (not real) good job. (Use an adverb to modify the adjective *good*.)

The addressee on this form is not a *real* person. (Use an adjective to modify the noun *person*.)

These engineers *surely* (not sure) can pose difficult questions. (Use an adverb to modify the verb *can pose*.)

He had a *firm* grip on the equipment. (Use an adjective to modify the noun *grip*.)

He gripped the equipment *firmly*. (Use an adverb to modify the verb *gripped*—how he gripped.)

OBJECTS OF THE VERB

Verbs may or may not have objects, but all *transitive* verbs have objects. These objects fall into one of two categories: *direct* or *indirect*. A *direct object* receives the action of the verb or shows the result of the action of the verb. The *indirect object* is the person or thing that receives a direct object. If you want to simplify the whole concept, remember that the direct object answers *what* about the verb and the indirect object tells *who* or *what received the direct object*.

Direct Objects

Michelle handles *complaints* so well that she has been promoted straight to heaven. (Michelle handles what?)

She is our fiction writer; she writes the *annual report*. (She writes what?)

The union pursues *problems* while they're still incidents. (The union pursues what?)

Our computer crunches *numbers* so well that we're thinking of upgrading its vitamins. (Our computer crunches what?)

Indirect Objects

io   do
My boss gave *me* the *privilege* of telling the president no. (My boss gave *who* [me—indirect object] *what* [privilege—direct object]?)

io   do
The president left my *boss* a *message* about where to

pick up his next check. (The president left *who* [boss—

indirect object] *what* [message—direct object]?)

Give our *department* the *break* that we deserve. (Give

who [department—indirect object] *what* [break—direct

object]?)

Can you show *Mack Nautiboy* the *signatures* on the

EEO lawsuit filed this morning? (Can you show *who*

[Mack Nautiboy—indirect object] *what* [signatures—

direct object]?)

COMPLEMENTS

Although a sentence is complete with only a subject and
a verb, a sentence may or may not have complements.
Again, complements fall into three categories: *subject
complements, object complements,* and *adjective complements.* (Forget about adjective complements until Chapter
4.) Subject complements tell more about the subject. Object complements tell more about the direct object. Subject
complements can be further divided into *predicate nouns*
or *predicate adjectives.*

If the complement *renames* the subject, the complement
is a *predicate noun.* If the subject complement *describes*
the subject rather than renames it, the subject complement
is a *predicate adjective.*

Subject Complement

> predicate noun (renames subject)
> predicate adjective (describes subject)

Object Complement
(describes or renames direct objects)

Subject Complements

Predicate Adjectives

Our marketing reps always feel *rejected*. (Describes *marketing reps*)

His buyers are *uninterested*. (Describes *buyers*)

The test results smell *fishy*. (Describes *results*)

The restrictions have become *intolerable*. (Describes *restrictions*)

Predicate Nouns

Curt Creativisky is the *originator* of our finance plan. (Renames *Curt Creativisky*)

This equipment, unfortunately, becomes a *heap* of junk as soon as the repairman leaves the premises. (Renames *equipment*)

Paper is *proof*. (Renames *paper*)

The grapevine news was top *secret* this morning. (Renames *news*)

Object Complements

Object complements tell more about direct objects.

He made the plan a *success* by having nothing to do with it. (Describes the direct object *plan*)

The boss appointed him chief *spokesman* without giving him a microphone. (Renames the direct object *him*)

Our in-house newsletter labeled the losses *"disappointing."* (Describes the direct object *losses*)

Our secretaries consider dictionaries a *waste* of time. (Renames the direct object *dictionaries*)

APPOSITIVES

An appositive directly follows and renames or further explains a noun or pronoun. The words that rename or explain are said to be "in apposition with" whatever they refer to.

My manager, *supervisor of the entire accounting function*, can't add or subtract but certainly knows how to intimidate creditors. (In apposition with *manager*)

He has expressed his position about alcohol and cafeteria food, *total abstinence*, to the entire staff. (In apposition with *position*)

The systems engineer, *Frank Doubletalk*, explained everything to the customer with enough acronyms and jargon to justify our billing. (In apposition with *engineer*)

NOTE: If you write "Frank Doubletalk, the systems engineer, explained . . . ," *Frank Doubletalk* becomes the subject, and *engineer* becomes the appositive.

NOUNS OF DIRECT ADDRESS

Sometimes the writer wants to address a comment to a person or group by name. The person or group addressed is the *noun of direct address*—as in "Hey, you."

Safety officers, in your investigative reports please make note of these bullet holes in the papaya plant.

Co-workers, I urge you to donate blood before they take it.

Simon Ripsnort, if you don't pay closer attention, the location of your next meeting will be the broom closet of our Siberian site.

EXPLETIVES

No, an expletive is not necessarily obscene language. Rather, an expletive is a word that has nothing grammatically to do with the rest of the sentence. The most frequent expletives are sentence beginnings such as *there is, there was, there were, there are, it is, it was.* Think of these beginnings as fillers without meaning.

> *There* were some problems with the decision. (*There* doesn't tell location. *There* doesn't say "six feet from the decision" we have problems. In this sentence *there* means nothing. The subject of the sentence is *problems*.)

> *It* is suggested that we leave early every Friday afternoon. (*It*, a meaningless subject, stands for the idea at the end of the sentence—*that we leave early every Friday afternoon*.)

MAJOR RELAPSES

The most frequent problems with sentence functions are misplaced modifiers and modifiers that do not modify at all; therefore, pay particular attention to how words relate to each other. Place modifiers as close to the words they describe as possible. Learn to ask yourself: What other word in the sentence does this specific word tell more about?

Incorrect:	This amount was under our projections because of incorrect assumptions about clearing and execution costs *by Marketing*. (*Costs* by Marketing? Or *assumptions* by Marketing?)
Correct:	This amount was under our projections because Marketing made incorrect assumptions about clearing and execution costs.

The best way to learn sentence functions is to visualize sentences. See the first few diagrams in Chapter 12 to cement the basic sentence functions in your mind before going on to Chapter 3.

THERAPY 2

In the following sentences, label each underlined word according to its sentence function. You have already had some practice in labeling verbs, adjectives, and adverbs in Chapter 1; in these instances, the part of speech is the same as the sentence function. Therefore, note that the adjective and adverb modifiers in these sentences are not underlined.

subject—s   subject complement—sc
verb (predicate)—v   object complement—oc
appositive—app   noun of direct address—nda
direct object—do   indirect object—io

NOTE: Don't worry that these sentences are too short and easy for good practice. In Chapters 3 and 4, we'll get to longer ones that are more similar to ones you write on the job. Concentrate on visualizing these sentences as you label each function. If you can't determine each sentence function, see the diagrams in Chapter 12 for help.

NOTE: The ✍ marks in the remainder of the book indicate sentences diagramed in Chapter 12.

1. Willetta Weightlossinzsky types Margaret Nospell-
   checker's audit reports.

2. ✍ My boss has been preparing his overdue resignation.

3. My price is cheap.

4. I will give you an answer today.

5. ✍ He considers team sports an unnecessary time-waster.

6. Douglas Donothing, a management consultant, sent the group a shocking invoice.

7. Margie, did you take this call?

8. There must be a problem.

9. Someone is always exercising his option clause.

10. ✍ These chemicals smell bad and taste poisonous.

11. She wants this job badly.

12. We produce junk mail here.

13. ✍ Candidly, the systems and design engineer, Muriel Hangover, made the project even more difficult.

14. His big sales orders sometimes generate very tiny bonuses and gigantic headaches.

15. You should never turn your unprotected back.

16. We did not take his phone message —his delaying tactic —Monday.

17. Both careful and careless writers should now recognize sentence functions.

18. Her pretty gray hair, George, does not necessarily represent wisdom.

19. Mistakes cost the department money and anger clients.

20. Take a good look at your corkboard.

21. We have arranged an incredibly innovative, phenomenally creative manufacturing process.

22. Boredom, an old excuse, is no excuse.

3

PHRASES

Grammar would be easy to learn if you could stop after Chapter 2, where all sentences are only a few words long. Grammar becomes more complex when, rather than having a single word in each function slot, sentences have entire phrases or clauses serving as subjects, direct objects, or whatever.

A phrase is a group of related words that does *not* contain both a subject and verb. This chapter will show you how to substitute phrases for single words.

He told his secretary the *news*. (Direct object)

He told his secretary *to leave Albert alone*. (A phrase substituting for a one-word direct object)

VERB PHRASES

Verb phrases are the easiest of all phrases to recognize. They consist of a verb plus the words that "help" the verb along. The most common helping words are parts of several verbs:

to be (is, are, was, were, am, be, being, been)	may, might, must
	shall, should
has, have, had	will, would
do, does, did	used to
can, could	ought to

Review the verb phrases in the following sentences:

I *have been asking* for a raise for the last three years.

My wife *has been nagging* me about not asking for a raise for the last ten years.

My boss *should have noted* my persistence all along.

My boss *does understand* my anger at the pittance paid me.

Our managers *are participating* in an annual review of performance and salaries.

I *may ask* about the raise again tomorrow.

But the company probably *will demand* more patience and better performance for my pittance.

Don't be confused about other parts of speech (usually adverbs) that interrupt a verb phrase:

Despite being an accountant, he *has* never thoroughly *understood* the terms "debit" and "credit." (*Never* and *thoroughly* are adverbs.)

Freda *is* apparently *approaching* retirement with great anticipation. (*Apparently* is an adverb.)

PREPOSITIONAL PHRASES

A prepositional phrase includes a preposition (*in, at, by, for, to, over*, etc.), its noun or pronoun object, and any modifiers. A prepositional phrase can function as an ordinary single-word adjective, adverb, or noun.

Prepositional Phrases As Adjectives

Remember that adjectives tell more about nouns or pronouns.

The announcement *for the class* arrived two days after the opening session. (*For the class* tells which announcement.)

The executive *in the picture* has her slip showing. (*In the picture* tells which executive.)

Prepositional Phrases As Adverbs

Remember that adverbs tell *when, where, why, how,* or *to what extent* about the verb, adjective, another adverb, or the sentence as a whole.

✍ He walked *into the conference room* with downcast eyes and open hands. (Where)

He altered the time card *during the morning break*. (When)

He adjusted the keyboard *with a hammer*. (How)

Prepositional Phrases As Nouns

Remember that nouns can act as subjects, direct objects, indirect objects, complements, appositives, objects of a preposition, or nouns of direct address.

✍ *In the winner's circle* is where I want to be. (The prepositional phrase substitutes as the subject of the sentence.)

My position, *in the middle,* will be advantageous in negotiating a settlement. (The prepositional phrase substitutes as an appositive, renaming *position.*)

She gave all the necessary information *to me.* (The prepositional phrase substitutes as an indirect object.)

NOTE: Remember that a direct object or indirect object can't be inside a prepositional phrase; instead, the entire prepositional phrase sits in the slot of the indirect object.

She gave *me* all the necessary information. (*Me*—indirect object)

VERBAL PHRASES

Don't confuse *verbal* phrases with *verb* phrases. Verb phrases show what a subject does, has, or is. Verbals are words that look like verbs but serve other purposes in the sentence. The three kinds of verbals are *participles, infinitives,* and *gerunds.* When these verbals include other modifying words, they become verbal phrases.

Participial Phrases

A participle is a verb ending in *-ing* or *-ed* that serves as an adjective. The participle and its related words form a participial phrase.

part
Tap dancing her way into the meeting, Hortense Hoffnangle took a seat as if no one had noticed her. (Describes *Hortense*)

The salesperson *waving the biggest banner* hasn't necessarily made the most sales. (Describes *salesperson*)

The *reduced* budget means another opportunity to build restraint in your employees. (Describes *budget*)

He drafted a resignation letter *lambasting everyone who had ever spoken to him in the halls*. (Describes *letter*)

The consultant's invoice, *listing expenses for everything from airfare to paper clips*, looks a little ridiculous. (Describes *invoice*)

A penny *saved* is a penny *lost to inflation*. (Both verbals describe *penny*. *Lost* is an irregular participle form because it does not end with -*ed* or -*ing*.)

Infinitive Phrases

An infinitive is the word *to* followed by a verb. An infinitive can serve as a noun, an adjective, or an adverb. The infinitive and its related words form an infinitive phrase.

As Noun

inf

To work with him is *to learn patience*. (Subject; subject complement)

inf

He wanted *to tell the client where he could get help*, but he thought better of it. (Direct object—tells *what* he wanted)

As Adverb

inf

He wrote a memo *to solicit funds for the Save-the-Snail Foundation*. (Tells *why* he wrote the memo)

inf

More and more people are using resumes *to fabricate a past* and *to create a future*. (Tells *how* people are using resumes)

As Adjective

inf

The decision *to eliminate holidays* met with a less-than-enthusiastic response. (Tells *which* decision)

inf

We have had an occasional problem with his tendency *to shout at customers*. (Tells *which* tendency)

Gerund Phrases

A gerund is a verb with an *-ing* ending that functions as a noun. A gerund and its related words form a gerund phrase.

gerund

Brady likes *getting a migraine headache* because he can leave work early enough to watch Monday-night football. (Substitutes as a direct object—Brady likes what?)

gerund

Tackling a project one step at a time overcomes procrastination only for those who don't tend to procrastinate anyway. (Substitutes as a subject)

gerund

He intends to win the sales award by *turning in duplicate orders*. (Substitutes as an object of the preposition *by*)

gerund

His suggestion is *writing off R & R on Cancun this year*. (Substitutes as a subject complement—a predicate noun that renames *his suggestion*)

NOTE: You may have noticed only a slight difference in some sentences between a participial phrase and a gerund phrase. The difference is emphasis. The participial construction emphasizes the doer; the gerund construction emphasizes the activity.

We noticed Claude *watching the cash drawer*. (Participial phrase—describes and emphasizes *Claude*)

We noticed *Claude's watching the cash drawer*. (Gerund phrase—emphasizes what Claude was doing. To understand why you must use a possessive form [like *Claude's*] before a gerund in this sentence, substitute a one-word noun in the slot: *We noticed Claude's attitude*.)

ABSOLUTE PHRASES

An absolute is a group of related words that has nothing grammatically to do with the rest of the sentence. In other words, the phrase doesn't clearly connect to or modify any particular word in the sentence. The phrase is like an "aside" comment. The word group differs from a clause in that it does not contain a verb (although it may contain a verbal).

This being the case, we completed the project and hopped on a plane for L.A. (You'll note that *this* is the subject of the word group; the verbal *being the case* tells more about *this*. The phrase doesn't connect to any other word in the sentence.)

My personal comfort the least of my concern, the employee lounge needs a few beds. (*My personal comfort the least of my concern* doesn't connect to or modify anything in the sentence.)

The CEO, *his mind made up*, appointed a subcommittee to study the standing committee to report back to the full committee. (*His mind made up* tells more about *the CEO*, but the phrase doesn't really connect to any part of the sentence.)

Speaking of contracts, where is the paperwork? (*Speaking of contracts* attaches to nothing specific in the sentence.)

Profits aside, I hate the buyer. (*Profits aside* attaches to nothing specific in the sentence.)

ELLIPTICAL PHRASES

Elliptical phrases refer to words that are missing (but understood) from the sentence. Frequently, elliptical phrases follow the words *as* or *than*. Sometimes the writer uses a comma to show that words are missing.

Whenever possible on this case, I want to practice honesty. (Whenever *it* is possible . . .)

I can cash this check immediately, if necessary. (. . . if *it is* necessary)

Bill Buffinknocker rides a bus to work; Joe Athlete, a bicycle. (. . . Joe Athlete *rides* a bicycle.)

While editing my boss's letters, I feel devilish. (While *I am* editing my boss's letters . ˙. .)

A hearty challenge, but is it a realistic one? (*It is* a hearty challenge . . .)

🖎 Overstatement is always more dangerous than understatement. (. . . more dangerous than understatement *is dangerous*)

We more frequently order our pencils from Petunia Office Supply than them. (We more frequently order our pencils from Petunia Office Supply than *we order pencils from* them.)

We order our pencils from Petunia Office Supply more often than they. (We order our pencils from Petunia Office Supply more often than they *order pencils from Petunia*.)

PARENTHETICAL PHRASES

Think of parenthetical phrases as those you normally set inside parentheses as an "aside." They usually interrupt the main clause to add nonessential information. Read the following sentences without the parenthetical phrases and note that the remaining words make a complete thought.

> Her attendance record, *to be sure*, does not make her the most dependable clerk in the organization. (This parenthetical phrase is also an infinitive phrase.)

> Our menu for the retirement luncheon, *not exactly extensive*, is the best we could manage for the $1.99/plate limit his boss imposed.

> What, *in your humble opinion*, is the cause of his haughty attitude? (This parenthetical phrase is also a prepositional phrase.)

MAJOR RELAPSES

Primarily, there are three ways to goof in substituting any of the foregoing phrases for single words: misplaced modifiers, dangling modifiers, and unparallel structure.

Misplaced Modifiers

To eliminate ambiguity, always place modifying phrases as close as possible to what they describe.

Incorrect:	*Lying flat on his back in the middle of the cafeteria,* the doctor examined the hemorrhaging employee. (The doctor was lying flat on his back?)
Correct:	Lying flat on his back in the middle of the cafeteria, the hemorrhaging employee was examined by the doctor.

Correct:	The doctor examined the hemorrhaging employee who was lying flat on his back.
Correct:	The hemorrhaging employee, lying flat on his back, was examined by the doctor.
Incorrect:	The receptionist refused to admit the visitor *with misgivings*. (Who had misgivings?)
Correct:	With misgivings, the receptionist refused to admit the visitor.
Incorrect:	Rip Ryhornberger thought *until October 1* we were still a subsidiary of MacIntosh Corporation. (Did he think until October 1?)
Correct:	Rip Ryhornberger thought we were still a subsidiary of MacIntosh Corporation until October 1.
Correct:	Rip Ryhornberger thought that until October 1 we were still a subsidiary of MacIntosh Corporation.

Dangling Modifiers

Be sure that a modifier correctly attaches to the word it describes. That is, does the modifier logically and clearly describe a specific, nearby word, phrase, or clause? The connection cannot simply be "understood."

Incorrect:	The rope was attached to the overhanging rock, hoping that it would hold the weight of the climber. (The rope hoped? *Hoping that it would hold the weight of the climber* doesn't "connect" to the person doing the hoping; in fact, whoever is hoping isn't even mentioned!)
Correct:	We attached the rope to the overhanging rock, hoping that it would hold the weight of the climber. (We hope.)

Incorrect:	To be as careful about the situation as possible, Harry's report should include step-by-step procedures. (Is Harry's report going to be careful?)
Correct:	To be as careful about the situation as possible, Harry should include step-by-step procedures in his report. (Harry will be careful.)
Incorrect:	By following these procedures, the process will take no time at all. (Does the process follow these procedures? No, a person follows the procedures.)
Correct:	If one follows these procedures, the process takes no time at all.
Incorrect:	Market sizes for the three geographical areas were estimated making a series of assumptions detailed in the proposal. (Heaven makes these assumptions?)
Correct:	Making a series of assumptions detailed in the proposal, I have estimated market sizes for the three geographical areas. (I made the assumptions.)

NOTE: Don't get confused about the understood "you." Modifiers must describe a specific person, thing, or idea *named* somewhere in the sentence. The only time *you* is understood is when you give commands such as: *Close the door.*

Be careful about dangling elliptical clauses that have both the subject and part of the verb omitted:

Incorrect:	While writing the accident report, the ambulance driver moved the body.
Correct:	While *I was* writing the accident report, the ambulance driver moved the body.
Correct:	While writing the accident report, *I saw* the ambulance driver move the body.

Parallelism Errors

Be sure to give equal ideas equal structure in your sentences:

Unparallel: *To be* or *not being*—that is the question. (The two ideas in equal slots do not balance.)

Parallel: *To be* or *not to be*—that is the question.

Unparallel: I know that Bob will find working with Henrietta Barrett *an enjoyable experience* and *worthwhile*.

Parallel: I know that Bob will find working with Henrietta Barett *an enjoyable* and *worthwhile* experience.

Unparallel: He prefers *leasing* or *to buy* the equipment.

Parallel: He prefers *to lease* or *to buy* the equipment.

Parallel: He prefers *leasing* or *buying* the equipment.

Unparallel: *Bad grammar* is like *having bad breath;* even your best friends won't tell you.

Parallel: *Bad grammar* is like *bad breath;* even your best friends won't tell you.

Parallel: *Using bad grammar* is like *having bad breath;* even your best friends won't tell you.

THERAPY 3

In each of the following sentences you will find one or more of the phrases we have discussed in this chapter: verbal phrases (participial, infinitive, or gerund), prepositional phrases, verb phrases, absolute phrases, elliptical phrases. The simple prepositions and verbals are italicized. Phrases within other phrases are shown as brackets within shading. Label each bracketed or shaded phrase. (Because you have already practiced identifying verb phrases, we have not bracketed those here.) When you find an elliptical phrase, write in the missing words.

participial phrase—part   infinitive phrase—inf
gerund phrase—gerund   prepositional phrase—prep
absolute phrase—abso   elliptical phrase—ell

1. *For* a change, Marguerita Marrymenot is not painting her nails *at* her desk.

2. The mistake *behind* him, Jasper Jazenspit has been promoted *to* vice president *in* charge *of* three-martini lunches.

3. *Coughing* loudly is cause *for* dismissal *around* his office.

4. Our salespeople have difficulty *deciding* whether *to phone* or *to write* potential customers *about* our new personally engraved pitchforks.

5. We know more than he knows *about* the problem *involving* his wife's phone calls.

6. *In* the meantime, we will supervise the *testing of our products to determine* durability and purpose.

7. An ounce *of* prevention can be much more expensive than a pound *of* cure.

8. Creativity *being minimal in* the company, I think we must have hired all left-brained people.

9. He pretends *to be* deaf *at* the whisper *of increased salaries in* the budget.

10. *Belonging to* the health club allows one *to learn* the bare essentials.

11. He's so lazy that we have *to include* a self-addressed envelope *to persuade* him *to mail* his insurance claims.

12. *To win* an argument *with* a customer is *to lose* a sale.

13. You could die *from* rheumatoid arthritis while ~~waiting in line at the copier~~.

14. The only way *to get* a vacation is *to make* a mistake or *to contract* typhoid.

15. *Forgetting* the past, we work *toward* Friday.

CLAUSES

Now that you know all about words and phrases, you have one more layer of information to learn: clauses. A clause differs from a phrase in that a clause is a group of related words, having a subject and a verb. (Remember: A phrase is a group of related words with no subject and verb.) The subjects and verbs in the following sentences are underlined.

His <u>signature</u> <u>can stop</u> this meeting.

Your <u>face</u> <u>would stop</u> a clock.

The <u>IRS</u> <u>audited</u> us for twenty consecutive years.

Interest <u>rates</u> and <u>bonds</u> <u>rise</u> and <u>fall</u> regardless of my discretionary income.

Clauses can substitute in a sentence for any single-word noun, pronoun, adjective, or adverb.

Bill is stupid. (A single-word subject)

Altering the contract is stupid. (A phrase as subject)

That he signed the contract is stupid. (A clause as subject)

The CIA recommends *him*. (A single-word direct object)

The CIA recommends *raising the payment*. (A phrase as direct object)

The CIA recommends *that you leave the country*. (A clause as direct object)

Send the bomb for *protection*. (A single-word object of the preposition)

Send the bomb by *mailing the entire camouflaged package*. (A phrase as object of the preposition)

Send the bomb by *whoever enters the building at noon*. (A clause as object of the preposition. *Whoever*—not whomever—is the subject of the verb *enters*).

He accessed our database *illegally*. (A single-word adverb telling how)

He accessed our database *in the early morning hours*. (A prepositional phrase as an adverb telling when)

He accessed our database *before we issued security clearance*. (A clause as an adverb telling when)

The *gargantuan* office shows a marked lack of good taste. (A single-word adjective)

The office *intended to create an aura of respect for our president* shows a marked lack of good taste. (A phrase as adjective)

The office *that Goldfinger wants* shows a marked lack of good taste. (A clause as adjective)

MAIN CLAUSES

Main clauses have a subject and a verb and express a complete thought. When a sentence contains two main clauses, the clauses are joined by one of seven conjunctions: *and, but, or, for, nor, so, yet.* If a conjunction is missing, the two clauses can be joined with a semicolon. The subject and verb in each of the following clauses are underlined.

In our next mail delivery we will be providing you with new wastebasket material. (One main clause)

Glenda Greetcher and her physician prepared the proposal calling for improved breathing conditions. (One main clause)

Our advertising campaigns usually draw nothing but bugs. (One main clause)

Your camera-ready art should be in our office at least ten minutes before press time. (One main clause)

I walked into his office to demand a promotion, and as a result of my persuasive presentation, he granted me a decrease in salary. (Two main clauses)

He <u>gathers</u> the forms together, <u>he</u> <u>throws</u> his rubber stamp toward them, and then <u>he</u> <u>signs</u> your name. (Three main clauses. The commas divide the three clauses, each of which can stand alone as a sentence.)

SUBORDINATE CLAUSES

A *subordinate clause* has a subject and a verb but does *not* express a complete thought by itself. A subordinate clause depends on, and in some way attaches to, a main clause for its complete meaning. A subordinate clause is introduced with a relative pronoun (such as *who, that, which*), a subordinate conjunction (such as *if, although, because*), or a connective adverb (such as *why, whenever, before*).

Tell *whoever wants to attend the convention* that *all speakers will bore them to tears*. (*Whoever* [not *whomever*] is the subject of the verb *wants*.)

Whoever wants to attend the convention doesn't make sense alone, but it is a clause because it contains a subject and a verb. Likewise, *that all speakers will bore them to tears* doesn't make sense alone, but it is a clause because it contains a subject and a verb.

Tell his *secretary* the *news*. (*Secretary*—indirect object; *news*—direct object)

Tell *whoever wants to attend the convention* that *all speakers will bore them to tears*. (First italicized clause —indirect object; second italicized clause—direct object. Tell who what?)

Subordinate Adjective Clauses

An adjective clause takes the place of a single-word adjective. In other words, an adjective clause describes a noun or a pronoun.

Let's take on a project *that will give us ample opportunity to show our skills in procrastination.* (*That will give us ample opportunity to show our skills in procrastination* tells more about *project*.)

Give this calendar with the 15th and 30th marked in red to the person *who will deliver your next paycheck.* (*Who will deliver your next paycheck* tells which person.)

He gave me two brochures about your soap, *which I have read thoroughly.* (*Which I have read thoroughly* tells more about the brochures.)

Harry, *who has played the role of mentor and has given me a broad knowledge of the entire business*, now plans to retire and take me with him into obscurity. (*Who has acted as my mentor and has given me a broad knowledge of the entire business* describes *Harry*.)

Subordinate Adverbial Clauses

An adverbial clause can substitute for a single-word adverb. That is, an adverbial clause tells when, where, how, or to what extent.

He can write the report *however he chooses.* (*However he chooses* substitutes for a one-word adverb telling how: He can write the report *sloppily*.)

She will get a raise *as soon as she persuades me.* (*As soon as she persuades me* substitutes for a one-word adverb telling when: She will get a raise *tomorrow*.)

We make the delivery *wherever they will accept the C.O.D. charges.* (*Wherever they will accept the C.O.D.*

charges substitutes for a one-word adverb telling where: We make the delivery *here*.)

He dictates his correspondence *because he never learned to spell*. (*Because he never learned to spell* substitutes for an adverbial prepositional phrase telling why: He dictates his correspondence *for protection*.)

You should never look your customer in the eye *when you ask her to sign the paperwork*. (*When you ask her to sign the paperwork* substitutes for a one-word adverb telling when: You should never look your customer in the eye *then*.

Subordinate Noun Clauses

A noun clause can substitute for any single-word noun —as a subject, direct object, indirect object, subject complement, object complement, object of a preposition, or adjective complement.

Tell the manager *where he can get the information*. (*Where he can get the information* substitutes for a single-word direct object: Tell the manager *your decision*.)

Although the fence wasn't too high, I suggest *that you have overstepped your bounds of authority*. (*That you have overstepped your bounds of authority* substitutes for a single-word direct object: I suggest *marketing*. Note that the first subordinate clause *although the fence wasn't too high* is an adverbial clause.)

That the $10,000 has been stolen is a matter of slight concern to me. (*That the $10,000 has been stolen* substitutes for a single-word subject: *The money* is a matter of slight concern to me.)

I will lend my welcome speech to *whoever likes the guy well enough to introduce him*. (*Whoever likes the guy well enough to introduce him* substitutes for a single-word object of the preposition *to*: I will lend my wel-

come speech to *Frances*. *Whoever* [not *whomever*] is
the subject of *likes*.)

Some employees may find *that they get paid half of
what they think they are worth and twice what the boss
thinks they are worth*. (*That they get paid half of what
they think they are worth and twice what the boss thinks
they are worth* takes the place of a one-word direct object: Some employees may find *conflict*. Note that this
noun clause has several smaller clauses inside it.)

I am glad *that you listed all your neuroses on the application*. (*That you listed all your neuroses on the application* completes the meaning of the adjective *glad*.
This clause is a complement of an adjective.)

MAJOR RELAPSES

You may get confused in four ways when substituting
clauses for words or phrases: incorrect punctuation,
phrases mistaken for clauses, clauses mistaken for sentences, and interrupted or inverted clauses.

Incorrect Punctuation

The way you punctuate a sentence depends on your understanding of subordinate and main clauses. You have to
be able to visualize the slot where a subordinate clause sits
inside a main clause. We will get to punctuation rules later;
for now, simply learn to distinguish between the two kinds
of clauses—main and subordinate.

Phrases Mistaken for Clauses

Remember that clauses must have a subject and a verb.
Phrases are often mistaken for clauses and are sometimes
treated as complete sentences. For example, the following
are phrases, not clauses:

To make you aware of the problem. (No verb. *To make* is an infinitive. What will make you aware of the problem?)

Being of sound mind and wishy-washy heart. (No subject. Who is *being?*)

That being the case for the interim period of the project. (No verb. *Being* is a participle describing *that.*)

Clauses Mistaken for Sentences

Main clauses express a complete thought; subordinate clauses do not. The following are clauses because they have a subject and a verb, but they are *not* sentences:

Clause:	Because the customer could not get an appropriate answer from the support center.
Sentence:	He called because the customer could not get an appropriate answer from the support center.
Clause:	However we choose to invoice for the services.
Sentence:	However we choose to invoice for the services will be fine with the client.

Interrupted or Inverted Clauses

To visualize separate clauses, restate to yourself the idea of the sentence in the most frequently used sentence order —subject, verb, object/complement:

What do you think is his main pain in closing the deal?

(*You do think what is* his main pain in closing the deal?

Or: *You do think* [that] his main pain in closing the deal *is* what?)

Tell me, if you have access to the information, who
                                              s   v
made this stupid decision. ([you] *Tell* me *who made* this
                            s   v
stupid decision if you *have* access to the information.
           s   v   s   v
Or: If *you have* access to the information, [you] *tell* me
  s   v
who made this stupid decision.)

                                           s v
The merger, I've been told, eliminates your job. (*I've*
  v   v   s   v
been told [that] the *merger eliminates* your job.)

THERAPY 4

In the following sentences underline the main clauses.
Put parentheses around the subordinate clauses. Label the
subordinate clauses either *adjective, adverb,* or *noun.* If
you have difficulty visualizing these clauses, review the
diagrams in Chapter 12.

1. ✍ These provisions are strictly enforced by the
                          adj. clause
   company, (which from time to time exercises its
   right to do stupid things).

2. Strafford told me the truth, but I prefer lies.

3. We want to silence our talking plants before they
   give away our top secrets.

4. The blue-eyed blonde is the customer who asked for a delivery date to coincide with her divorce.

5. As he left the 56th floor, I left the building.

6. When it is time to go to lunch, wake me.

7. I explained how easily small computers fit into briefcases.

8. Can you tell me why you chose a mauve-colored lavatory?

9. The director's nose twitches when the subject of taxes surfaces.

10. Let me explain profits to you: products go out, and money comes in.

11. Sue Snitt and Dwardon Blum reiterated our goals and then sabotaged our efforts to reach them.

12. Don't simply display the product; ask for his purchase order number.

13. We believe that you share the company's concern about rising prices and lower incentive awards.

14. We would like to know where you got the inside information.

15. The security code that was cracked is supposed to be foolproof; what does that make you?

16. The construction cost is ridiculous when you compare it to any other bid.

17. I suggest that you consider the possibility of your being fired over the issue.

18. ✍ Tell me how you sold that merchandise, and I'll tell you how I figured your commission.

19. As soon as the doctor diagnoses Mr. Comunglued's

psychosis, the boss will tell you how to handle that customer.

20. Psychotic behavior is how he avoids the tough assignments.

21. The security officers looked askance at the size of my briefcase.

22. The security officers asked why I made so many trips in and out of the building with my briefcase.

23. The last supervisory course on avoiding sexual harassment involved role plays that required no acting at all on our part.

24. If the customer calls in the next few days before the warranty expires, put him on hold.

25. That the deadline is Friday doesn't seem to bother him.

SENTENCES

In the last chapter you learned that a clause has a subject and a verb. A subordinate clause cannot stand alone, but rather depends on the main clause to complete is meaning. A main clause expresses a complete thought. Therefore, a *sentence* must have at least one main clause because a sentence has a subject and verb and expresses a complete thought. A sentence may or may not have one or more subordinate clauses.

Sentences can be divided into four categories: *simple, compound, complex,* and *compound-complex.*

SIMPLE SENTENCES

A *simple sentence* contains one main clause and no subordinate clauses. The simple subjects and simple predicates (verbs) in the following sentences are underlined.

<u>Cheryl</u> <u>pouted</u>.

We <u>are writing</u> to acknowledge receipt of your stupid letter.

<u>Customers</u> sometimes <u>complain</u>.

<u>Haste</u> in getting products to market <u>can make</u> you healthy, wealthy, and wise.

To be very frank with you, <u>I know</u> very little about my job.

COMPOUND SENTENCES

A *compound sentence* contains two or more main clauses and no subordinate clauses. That is, all the clauses express a complete thought. All main clauses are joined by either a semicolon or one of these seven coordinate conjunctions: *and, but, or, nor, for, so, yet.* In the following sentences, each main clause is italicized; the simple subjects and simple predicates (verbs) are underlined.

<u>We</u> <u>do</u> not <u>train</u> our employees; <u>we</u> <u>program</u> them.

<u>I</u> <u>wanted</u> to finish the project ahead of schedule, so <u>we</u> <u>sent</u> our manager out to buy paper clips.

🖐 *<u>He</u> <u>practiced</u> the presentation thoroughly, <u>he</u> <u>prepared</u> the proper visuals,* and *then <u>he</u> <u>pulverized</u> the main points before his top-management audience.*

You can lead an employee to the computer, but *you cannot make him crunch the right numbers.*

To stay within our budget at luncheons, they have substituted *anchovies for caviar as an appetizer,* and we are serving *prime tuna instead of prime rib as the entree.*

COMPLEX SENTENCES

A *complex sentence* contains one main clause and at least one subordinate clause. In the following sentences, the main clauses are italicized; the subordinate clauses are inside parentheses or brackets. Notice that sometimes the subordinate clause sits inside the main clause. These subordinate clauses are occupying a single-word slot as a subject, adverb, or whatever. The simple subjects and simple predicates (verbs) of each clause are underlined.

(When you apply for an exemption), *you must have a personnel file detailing every activity since birth.*

(If at first your secretary succeeds), *promote her to manager.* (The "you" subject of the main clause is understood.)

He terminated the project (when the results began to look bleak).

Darla Drastic, (who knows nothing about oil and gas),
has become president of Petroleum International.

This is to advise you (that our files contain much unnecessary paperwork).

🖎 *She did not get a raise* (because she had the nerve
to think [that she deserved it]).

NOTE: Complex sentences can be confusing when the
subordinate clause sits inside a main clause. You learned
that a main clause has a subject and a verb and expresses a
complete thought by itself. That definition of a main clause
can be foggy with a sentence such as the following (but,
alas, it's the best we grammarians can do):

That you want to sell the product is not exactly a surprise.

That you want to sell the product is a subordinate clause
serving as a subject of the main clause. In other words, a
sentence such as this cannot be easily divided into two
parts such as the following one:

sub clause	main clause
If you sell the product,	I will be surprised.

Nevertheless, even when the main clause must have the
subordinate clause inside it to make sense, sentences such
as the following are complex sentences.

A bonus is *what he expects*.
That you object to his plan will not bother him.

What you know and *what you do* are not as important as *who invites you to play golf* and *who knows your father*.

COMPOUND-COMPLEX SENTENCES

A *compound-complex sentence* contains at least two main clauses (which make it compound) and at least one subordinate clause (which makes it complex). In the following sentences, the main clauses are italicized; the subordinate clauses are within parentheses. Again, notice that the subordinate clauses often sit inside the main clauses. These subordinate clauses are occupying a single-word slot as a direct object, subject, adjective, or whatever. All the simple subjects and simple predicates (verbs) of each clause are underlined:

[(If Harry is sure of his decision)], *he should write a memo to the file*, and *then he should tell his secretary to misfile it for a couple of weeks*.

Martha has ghostwritten the report, but *Jack's supervisor has full knowledge of the situation* (because I told him).

Our records indicate (that no one here officially hired him,) but *he keeps showing up for work every morning*.

We are unable to refund your money; however, (if you have any further questions) *please call me* (so that we can refuse to answer).

✍ (If the equipment works well on the drawing board), *it will work spasmodically* (when you make a presentation to management); *it will not work at all* (when you demonstrate it to the customer).

I make the little decisions in our department, such as (how we spend the money), (whom we hire), *and* (what products we manufacture); *my boss makes the big decisions, such as* (how we best can persuade Congress to pay off the national debt) *and* (how we can prepare for nuclear war).

(How I travel to work) *and* (where I eat my lunch) *are my business, but* (what I do) (while I'm here) *is nobody's business*.

We request (that you please furnish us with a certified copy of your birth certificate); *we will need indisputable proof of your birth*.

To visualize sentence patterns, study the following examples. Main clauses are italicized. Subordinate clauses are in regular type.

Simple Sentence

I resigned.

Compound Sentence

I resigned, but I know Dave.

Complex Sentence

I resigned before Dave joined the company.

Compound-Complex Sentences

I resigned before Dave joined the company, *but I know him.*

I resigned before Dave joined the company, but I know him because his wife sued me for child support.

Simple Sentence

Philippa drove her point into the ground.

Compound Sentence

Philippa drove her point into the ground, and she was successful.

Complex Sentence

Philippa drove her point into the ground after the meeting ended.

Compound-Complex Sentences

Philippa drove her point into the ground after the meeting ended, *and she was successful.*

Philippa drove her point into the ground after the meeting ended, *and she was successful* because she used her head.

MAJOR RELAPSES

Fragments

The major mixup in identifying sentence patterns is that some writers mistake a subordinate clause for a complete sentence. Instead of a sentence, they write a *fragment*.

Fragment:	He came in out of the rain. Because her supervisor told him to do so.
Sentence:	He came in out of the rain because her supervisor told him to do so.
Fragment:	Although we have given him hundreds of orders in the past.
Sentence:	Although we have given him hundreds of orders in the past, he still expects payment on this new one.

Incorrect Punctuation

Recognizing various kinds of clauses and sentence patterns is essential to determining correct punctuation. Simply take my word for that at this point, and we'll get to punctuation rules in Chapter 9.

Insubordination

Clauses can show insubordination as well as employees can. Many people have the careless habit of joining two ideas in a sentence with a common linking word such as *and* or *but*. However, you should use *and, but*, or *or* only to join equal ideas.

In addition, always examine each sentence containing two unequal ideas to decide which is the major idea and which is the minor idea. Always place the minor idea in the subordinate clause and the major idea in the main clause. Notice correct placement of major and minor ideas in Therapy 5. Finally, be cautious about the subordinate conjunctions *since*, *while*, and *as*.

To avoid ambiguity, do not use *since* to mean *because*:

Because (not since) he has talked with the lawyer, we have decided they are serious. (With *since*, the sentence can refer to time— *since the day he talked with the lawyer*.)

To avoid ambiguity, do not use *while* to mean *although*:

Although (not *while*) I don't have all the answers, I do know the questions. (With *while*, the sentence can mean *during the time I don't have the answers*.)

To avoid ambiguity, do not use *as* to mean *because*:

He cannot finish the report this week *because* (not *as*) he is flying to Peru. (With *as*, the sentence can mean that he cannot finish the report *during* his flight. But what about before or after he makes the trip?)

Some writers conclude that perhaps it's best to use only simple sentence patterns. In general, simple sentences are clear and emphatic. But the use of too many simple sentences makes your writing monotonous and the ideas choppy. With varied sentence patterns, you can connect your ideas logically and better help the reader follow your reasoning from thought to thought.

Choppy, monotonous:	Sue Smith worked for you in 1983. She gave your name as a reference. She applied for a job at Artex. You know about her customer-relations experience. We will appreciate your comments on her performance.
Improved:	Sue Smith, who worked for you in 1983, gave your name as a reference when she applied for a job at Artex. Because you know about her customer-relations experience, we will appreciate your comments on her performance.

THERAPY 5

Identify clauses and sentence patterns in the following sentences. Circle the simple subjects and simple predicates (verbs) of each clause. Underline main clauses, and place parentheses around subordinate clauses. Use brackets to show subordinate clauses inside subordinate clauses. In the margin, label the sentence patterns: simple, compound, complex, or compound-complex.

Complex   1. (If you like these notepads [that I ordered]]), I will plan to write you more notes on motivational mannerisms.

2. You may have to tie him with his own red tape to get him in the sales meeting.

3. If the lawsuit fits, settle out of court.

4. What the world needs now is a good $20 steak.

5. This consultant's project is an ongoing process; it will not end until all our budget has been exhausted.

6. Where we have given generous bonuses, we have also harnessed much brainpower.

7. Riding a horse to work saves gas and clears the freeways of traffic.

8. All our new employees attend an orientation session to learn to pronounce the boss's name.

9. Seniority around our office means that you have much patience and no backbone.

10. I wouldn't say that the meeting was a

long one, but we sent out our laundry.

11. It would appear that no one is in charge here.

12. Whoever laughs last is assigned the project.

13. Whoever has all the answers evidently does not understand all the questions.

14. Attached is the schedule showing what time you reported to work each morning last year; therefore, we trust that you have recorded the correct hours on your records also.

15. We have examined our files and have determined that you are currently exempt from receiving a paycheck.

16. Although I agree that your plan is an excellent idea, the system needs some refining.

17. We entered the product name for each new account, the customer number for each old account, the invoicing procedure for each division, the contact name and address for each order; thus, the report is consistent and brief.

18. We have emergency plans for all kinds of inclement weather, such as hurricanes, tornadoes, hailstorms, and nuclear fallout; there are no provisions for rain.

19. The trustees asked the committee to meet during the first quarter because of the confusion and cost of two separate billings, the decision of some residents not to subscribe to the ser-

vice, and the desire to be more specific about the expenses of the maintenance fund.

20. I asked Lawrence L. Lamkin to set up an appointment with his supervisor and me so that we could make some determination about his future with the company.

21. I asked Sara Hooper if it were true that she had been estimating the figures in our reports, and she stated that in a few instances when things did not add up she had altered the numbers.

22. Your representative has been briefed on these procedures and will be able to answer any questions you may have, as long as they are limited to price and availability.

23. All our retailers and distributors want motor-oil products that can be promoted at the price shown in the three ads running in today's paper, and as you know, this plan is not feasible because most of the sales people do not see the ads of their products.

24. We are unaware of any reason to withdraw the product from the market; but if you feel that you want a product that works, please let us know, and we will attempt to correct the difficulties.

25. Did you really expect this machine to work when you ordered it?

26. Please instruct your officers to review the credit files for current financial information, to provide all necessary information for the loan

application, and to delineate the strength of your credit position.

27. Unless you plan to appear before the board after an extended fast, your efficiency in making the presentation has little to do with management's acceptance of the idea that the company cafeteria should be subsidized.

28. Before leaving on vacation, please check with the personnel office to see if you will have a job when you return.

29. We think that your attendance at this meeting is a necessity, no matter how boring it is.

30. That he frowns when he hears the boss's name must mean that he has some recollection of his life before the head injury.

31. With the conclusion of this chapter, you know enough grammar terms to pass the state board exam for speakers of English.

6

AGREEMENT—PRONOUNS

Several things must agree (or match) within sentences: Verbs must agree in number with their subjects. Verb tenses must accurately reflect time. Clauses should be consistent in voice and mood.

In this first of the three chapters on agreement, we'll stick to pronoun agreement. Pronouns must agree in person, number, and gender with the nouns they replace. The case of a pronoun must be appropriate for the way a pronoun functions in the sentence (as a subject, direct object, indirect object, etc.)

PERSON, NUMBER, GENDER

Pronouns must agree in . . .

- person (first person—*I, we*; second person—*you*; third person—*she, they, one*)

- number (singular—*it, his*; plural—*they, we*)
- gender (masculine—*him*; feminine—*her*; neuter —*it*)

. . . with words they replace (their antecedents) in the sentence.

> The House plans to raise corporate taxes; *it* (not *they*) may add a tax for breathing. (*It* refers to *House*. Singular, neuter gender)

> The company *officers* consider the lawyer quite a wit; *they* are half right. (*They* refers to *officers*. Plural, neuter gender)

> *Hortense* assumes *she* can handle the work *herself*. (*She* and *herself* replace Hortense. Singular, feminine gender)

> Company policy states that everyone (not *you*) should wear safety gear while visiting that site. (Don't carelessly switch from third person to second: . . . *that you should wear* . . . , meaning *everybody* or *people* or *employees* should wear safety gear.)

Demonstrative pronouns are words that point out: *this, that, these, those*. These pronouns must agree in number with the noun that follows.

Singular	*Plural*
this announcement	these announcements
that handbook	those handbooks

FUNCTION (CASE)

Do you have trouble with sentences like these?

Bob explained the problem to Cheryl and (me or I?).

The problem really involves a technicality to be worked out between Tom Hornsby and (I or me?).

If so, you need to understand pronoun *case*.

You remember that sentence functions include subject, verb, adjective modifier, direct object, etc. Therefore, for pronouns to match their function appropriately means that only objective pronouns can sit in object slots (direct object, indirect object, and object of the preposition), and only nominative (subject) pronouns can sit in subject slots. Pronouns cannot be used interchangeably in an object slot and in a subject slot. To get technical, we say pronouns have *case*. That is, the pronoun *case* (or type) has to be appropriate to how the pronoun functions in the sentence.

Nominative Case

(Pronouns that serve as subjects)

I	you	he	she	it
we	they	who	whoever	

Subject of the verb

You need help fast.

We destroyed the project.

Whoever cares enough should speak up about the issue.

I do not know *who* answers the phone when *I* am away. (*I*—subject of *do know*; *who*—subject of *answers*; I—subject of *am*)

Appositive of the subject

Those who knew him, *we* on the third floor, favored his dismissal. (Further elaborates and renames *those who knew him*.)

	Nominative Case	Objective Case	Possessive Case
Singular Number			
First Person: (Speaking *of* yourself)	I	me	my, mine
Second Person: (Speaking *to* someone)	you	you	your, yours
Third Person: (Speaking *about* someone)	he, she, it, who, whoever	him, her, it, whom, whomever	his, her, hers, its, whose
Plural Number			
First Person: (Speaking *of* yourself and at least one other person)	we	us	our, ours
Second Person: (Speaking *to* more than one person)	you	you	your, yours
Third Person: (Speaking *about* more than one person)	they, who, whoever	them, whom, whomever	their, whose, theirs

Subject complement

The problem was *they* who signed off on the project. (*They* renames the subject *the problem*.)

Gloria Guttenheimer did the research; therefore, the expert is *she*, not *I*. (*She* and *I* rename the subject of the second clause, *expert*.)

Objective Case

(Pronouns that serve as objects)

me	you	him	her	it
us	them	whom	whomever	

Direct object

Please send *him* to Alaska for the winter.

Kick *him* upstairs, where the support group will appreciate his delaying tactics.

Indirect object

Give *her* the information Martha Meddlesome needs to fight the reprimand.

We have told *her* where to go with this assignment.

Object of the preposition

You can submit the report directly to *me*, and I'll make sure he approves the budget.

This report was written by *them*, and now they are rejecting its conclusions.

Appositive of an object

He instructed his team, Ruth and *me*, to ignore the project deadline. (In apposition with *team*, the indirect object)

Object of the infinitive

Ask him to give *us* the reason for the delay.

This invoice should help to persuade *them* that the problem is growing more serious by the second.

Subject of the infinitive

(That a *subject* of an infinitive must be an *objective-case* pronoun is a strange rule. All other subject functions require a nominative-case pronoun.)

We have told *them* to leave all unordered merchandise on the truck. (Subject of *to leave*)

NOTE: Don't use a reflexive or intensive pronoun (*myself, yourself, himself*) when you need a simple personal pronoun (*me, you, him*). A sentence must contain another pronoun or a noun to which the reflexive or intensive pronoun refers.

I *myself* did the interviewing. (Adds emphasis to *I*)

He canceled the meeting with John and me (not *myself*) because John had high fever with his temper tantrum.

(No special emphasis. Drop the name and your ear will help you choose correctly: *He canceled the meeting with me*.)

He presented the proposal to Bob Shaggard and me (not *myself*). (No special emphasis. Drop the name and your ear will help you choose correctly. *He presented the proposal to me*.)

Wyatt Hooker and he (not *himself*) told the department manager about the layoffs. (No special emphasis. Drop the name and your ear will help you choose correctly: *He told the department manager about the layoffs*.)

Possessive Case

(Pronouns that show ownership)

my	her	our
mine	hers	their
your	its	theirs
yours	our	whose
his		

This briefcase is *mine; hers* is the one with the trap lid.

His proposals are preposterous, and that's why the consultants are enthralled about *their* own implementation plan.

NOTE: Always use possessive-case pronouns before gerunds.

The essence of the problem centers around *his* (not *him*) delaying the announcement. (The problem does not center around *him* delaying; it centers around *his delaying*. Remember that the gerund phrase *delaying the announcement* sits in the slot of a single-word noun. To understand why you need a possessive form before a gerund, try substituting another noun for the gerund in the sentence above: The essence of the problem centers around his *approach*.)

MAJOR RELAPSES

Be careful to choose nominative-case pronouns to fit the subject slots of a sentence and objective-case pronouns to fit object slots of a sentence. The most common mistake with pronouns is to use a subject pronoun in an object slot.

Incorrect: Just between you and *I*, I think the project will fail. (*I* sits in the slot of an object of the preposition *between*. Therefore, you need the objective-case pronoun *me*.)

Incorrect: Ask Jim and *I* for whatever equipment you need for the sales hoopla. (*I* sits in the slot of a direct object. Therefore, you need the objective-case pronoun *me*.)

The easiest way to choose the correct pronoun is to omit the other people named in the sentence. Then trust your ear.

The customer set up the conference call with Bucky Buckwheat and me to discuss plans for an earlier delivery date. (*The customer set up the conference call with me to discuss plans for an earlier delivery date.*)

We managers like the idea. (Drop *managers: We like the idea.*)

Tell *us* managers about the idea. (Drop *managers: Tell us about the idea.*)

Here are two other tips for using *who* and *whom* correctly. 1) Substitute *he* or *him* for *who* or *whom* in the sentence to let your ear help you choose. *He* and *who* are "subject" words; *him* and *whom* are "object" words. (The one exception is a subject of an infinitive.) 2) Restructure the sentence in your mind so that you can clearly see how the *who, whoever, whom,* or *whomever* serves in the sentence.

Give this job to *whom?* (Object of preposition—Give this job to *him?*)

Who will make the final decision? (Subject of *will make* —*He* will make the final decision.)

We have phoned the office manager, *who* we believe will correct the situation today. (Subject of *will correct* —We believe *he/who* will correct the situation today.)

We have phoned the office manager, *whom* we like. (Direct object—We like *him/whom.*)

THERAPY 6

Correct the pronoun errors in the following sentences. Explain your answers by identifying how the pronoun functions in each sentence (subject, appositive of a subject, subject complement, direct object, indirect object, object of a preposition, object of an infinitive, appositive of an object, subject of an infinitive). Remember this tip: Omit

the other people named in the sentence and then trust your
ear for the correct pronoun choice.

1. I have been advised by Sam Sledgehammer, Jody
                    him (obj. of preposition *by*)
   Jaggernut, and ~~he~~ about the situation developing
   with the basement flooding.

2. Tutty Taylor, Tarzan Tamerick, and myself all
   brought the matter to his attention.

3. Tell whomever answers the phone that the boss is in
   conference and cannot take the call.

4. Your marketing representative can arrange for
   Marge Guttenheimer or I to contact you before Friday for last-minute details.

5. Our president, Helen Garter, has reviewed your resume, along with those of students from several
   other universities. As a result, her and I have selected several candidates for further interviews; you
   are not one of them.

6. If you have any questions, please don't ask Joanne, Bubba, Binky, or I for answers.

7. The attorney explained all the details of the settlement to whomever called his office on Friday.

8. Address this complaint about the purple carpet to who?

9. The supervisors, us in this office included, have already kissed all the babies we intend to kiss.

10. My manager, who I consider antagonistic, holds the purse strings to my future dress-for-success look.

11. The operation involves several department heads from Dallas—Tom Jones, Mike Sparks, and I—as well as those from Atlanta.

12. I fired him, although he is a person who I respect.

13. By phoning the support center or myself personally,
    you can get any information you need.

14. Let me know if John or him can conduct the inter-
    views for belly dancers.

15. He asked that they write Wade Johnson or I about
    the agreement.

7

AGREEMENT—SUBJECTS AND VERBS

Subjects and verbs must agree in number. That is, singular subjects take singular verbs, and plural subjects take plural verbs. Don't get confused by -s endings. Remember that *nouns* ending in -s or -es are usually plural, but *verbs* ending in -s or -es are usually singular.

SINGULAR	*PLURAL*

Nouns

car	cars
typewriter	typewriters
report	reports

Verbs

the reporter says	reporters say
he writes	we write
she disagrees	they disagree

Some forms of the verb do not show whether they are singular or plural. In other words, whether referring to one person or sixteen, some verb forms remain the same.

SINGULAR	*PLURAL*
I *can wait*	We *can wait*
A report *must reveal*	Reports *must reveal*

COLLECTIVE NOUNS

A collective noun names people, things or ideas as a group: *staff, committee, management, audience, group, equipment, company.* Most collective nouns in business writing are singular.

Management disagrees with whatever we propose. (*Management* is acting as a collective group.)

My *staff helps* with complex situations in that department. (*My staff* is a collective group.)

If the collective noun refers to several of a group individually, however, the verb should be plural.

The *audience whisper* among themselves each time the manager mentions plans for the Christmas party at Ernie's Deli.

The *committee argue* among themselves on every decision they make.

Sentences with collective nouns such as these sound better if reworded:

The *members of the audience* whisper among themselves each time the manager mentions plans for the Christmas party at Ernie's Deli.

The *committee members* argue among themselves on every decision they make.

PLURAL IN FORM BUT SINGULAR IN MEANING

Some subjects plural in form but singular in meaning take a singular verb:

Economics is a subject few directors understand well enough to make their companies profitable in times of recession.

Hives is a good way to prove your frustration over the assignment in Saudi Arabia.

The *news* from his office *is* always depressing.

Research and development is his area of responsibility.

Some subjects plural in form but singular in meaning take a plural verb:

The *premises have been* thoroughly *inspected*.

My *thanks go* to each of you who makes me look literate.

His *savings were depleted* years ago.

EXPRESSIONS OF TIME, MONEY, AND QUANTITIES

When thought of as a single unit, expressions of time, money, and quantity take a singular verb.

Ten dollars is actually quite inexpensive for the kind of coffee I ordered.

Two hours is enough time to draft a resignation letter and clear out your desk.

Four acres in the country has become his idea of retirement.

COMPOUND SUBJECTS

Subjects linked equally with *and* (called *compound subjects*) take a plural verb.

Jack and *Jill* have gone up Washington's hill to get an explanation of the new policy.

What he says and *what he does* are never consistent.

NOTE: Be sure that you have a true compound subject before making the verb plural. Nouns or pronouns introduced after the subject with phrasal prepositions such as *as well as, along with, in addition to, rather than, including, accompanied by,* and *together with* are not part of the subject. They are subordinate to, not equal to, the subject.

The *vice president,* together with three managers from Fresno, *is* responsible for the project. (*Together with three managers from Fresno* is not part of the subject. But: *The vice president and three managers from Fresno* is a compound subject and requires a plural verb.)

NOTE: Subjects connected by *and* but preceded by *each, every, many a,* or *many an* require a singular verb.

Every man, woman, and child *is* discriminated against in our store.

Many an engineer *has been fired* for less than what you've done.

EITHER/OR—NEITHER/NOR—NOT ONLY/BUT ALSO

Consider both halves of *either/or* and *neither/nor* subjects as if they are separate elements. Subjects linked by *either/or* and *neither/nor* usually take a singular verb. If one subject is plural and the other subject is singular, make the verb agree with the closest subject. Unless there is reason not to do so, prefer writing the plural subject second because the construction sounds less awkward.

Either *Heidi Headhooper* or *Hilda Hildabrand* has garbled your message.

Not only *bicycling* but also *sailboating* is being planned for the company's Memorial Day picnic.

Neither *Clyde's report* nor *the reports we received from the Ohio office* have contained an iota of truth. (The second subject of the pair, *the reports we received from the Ohio office*, requires a plural verb.)

THE UNDERSTOOD "YOU"

You may be expressly stated as the subject of a sentence or *you* may be understood:

Please review these reports, and give me your comments by Friday.

Ask not what we can pay you; ask what you can contribute to the profit picture.

Even when *you* is expressed, *you* may be either singular or plural in meaning but always requires a plural verb.

You are tempting me to resign. (One person or several people)

INVERTED SENTENCE ORDER

Most English sentences follow one of two patterns: subject-verb-object or subject verb complement. When you structure a sentence in an unusual (inverted) order, be sure to identify the subject before making the verb either singular or plural.

Also confusing about these proposals *was* the *statement* that the merchandise would not be available until 1996. (The subject *statement* follows the verb. *Proposals* is the object of the preposition *about*.)

In his written elaborations about the remodeling plans and the color schemes *is* only one *hint* of the exorbitant cost. (The subject *hint* follows the verb. *Elaborations*, *plans*, and *schemes* are objects of prepositions.)

INDEFINITE PRONOUNS

Verbs after indefinite pronouns such as *none*, *most*, *all*, *some*, *more*, and *any* agree with the context of the sentence. That is, these pronouns can be singular or plural depending on what noun or pronoun they replace or refer to in the context of the passage.

Some of the money *is missing*. (Singular—*Some* refers to *money*)

Some of the coins *are missing*. (Plural—*Some* refers to *coins*.)

None of the equipment *has been damaged*. (Singular—*None* refers to equipment.)

None of the machines *are* working. (*None* can mean *not one* or *not any.* Also correct: *None* of the machines *is working.*)

None of those who care about the project *are concerned* about their paychecks.

Most of my time *is spent* hiding from the boss. (Singular—*Most* refers to *time.*)

Most of my colleagues *understand* how to survive in this environment. (Plural—*Most* refers to *colleagues.*)

SEPARATED SUBJECTS AND VERBS

In longer sentences agreement can become confusing when other words, phrases, or clauses come between the subject and the verb.

One of the lesser-known training programs that would solve your problems *has been ignored.*

Confusion about policy statements, vacation schedules, and restroom facilities *creates* a sense of urgency.

VERB COMPLEMENTS

In sentences containing linking verbs (*is, was, becomes, appears,* etc.) you sometimes have a plural subject and a singular complement or vice versa. In such cases, always make the verb agree with the subject, not the complement.

Radial *tires are* the product we want to push this month.

The *product* we want to push this month *is* radial tires.

The trial *balance is* the credits and debits.

The *credits and debits are* the trial balance.

One of the primary considerations *is* the typographical errors in the brochure.

The typographical *errors are* our primary consideration.

NOTE: With awkward-sounding constructions, try to re-word the sentence.

The radial *tire is* the *product* we want to push this month.

One of the primary consideration *is* the *matter* of typographical errors in the brochure.

RELATIVE PRONOUNS AS SUBJECTS

A relative pronoun such as *who, that,* or *which* has no number within itself; the noun the pronoun replaces determines whether the corresponding verb should be either singular or plural.

He planned the total program, *which is* boring to every-one who attends. (*Which* refers to *program*; therefore, the verb that follows *which* is singular.)

He planned all the programs, *which are* boring to every-one who attends. (*Which* refers to *programs*; therefore, the verb that follows *which* is plural.)

My competitor delivered samples of a product *that du-plicates* what we have in development. (The verb after *that* is singular when *that* stands for *product*.)

My competitor delivered samples of a product *that du-plicate* the samples we already have. (The verb after *that* is plural when *that* stands for *samples*.)

This is *one* of the public-relations functions *that is* un-derbudgeted. (This one function out of a group of functions is underbudgeted.)

This is one of the public-relations *functions that are* underbudgeted. (This function is one of several under-budgeted PR functions.)

SPECIAL CASES

Latin Words

One special case is the Anglicizing of foreign words such as *data/datum, criteria/criterion, media/medium*. With the last two pairs, we have kept the distinction between singular and plural. However, *datum*, the singular of *data*, has become archaic now; *data* can be either singular or plural. Note the difference in meaning in these sentences:

Our *data* show this to be the best approach. (Plural verb—several pieces of information)

Our *data* shows this to be the best alternative. (Singular verb—our collective body of information)

Fractions/Percentages/Portions

Another special case is the use of fractions, percentages, or other words that mean part of a whole. Choose a plural verb when the sentence implies a plural noun or when a plural noun follows. Choose a singular verb when the sentence implies a singular noun or when a singular noun follows.

One-half of the mailing list *has been accidentally deleted.* (Singular—refers to *list*)

One-fourth of the booklets *have* missing pages. (Plural —refers to the booklets individually)

The *majority* of our employees *commute* to work by airplane. (Plural—refers to individual employees)

A clear *majority favors* the acquisition. (Singular—a group)

Seventy percent of my time *is spent* in this building. (Singular—refers to *time*)

Twenty percent of my employees *are* eager to leave. (Plural—refers to *employees*)

Part of our plans *have* materialized. (Plural—refers to *plans*)

Part of our office *is being remodeled*. (Singular—refers to *office*)

Sixty percent of our typists *have* excellent skills. (Plural—refers to typists individually)

Sixty percent of the group *has* a hundred percent of the money. (Singular—refers to the group collectively)

A Number/The Number

A *number* of people *have called* to tell you where to go. (Plural—meaning *several* people)

The number of people who are unhappy working here *is growing* every payday. (Singular—meaning a specific total)

Positive and Negative Subjects

When a sentence has both a positive and negative subject, make the verb agree with the positive subject.

The three *managers* and not the technician *are* running this show.

My *hunch* and not your crazy numbers *is* what I plan to base my decision on with regard to next year's budget.

MAJOR RELAPSES

Although on occasion you may "write by ear," you can't trust your ear (or instinct) with subject-verb agreement. Particularly dangerous is trusting your ear on verbs that go with dependent clauses introduced by *which* or *that*. Because *which* or *that* as subjects can replace either singular or plural nouns, be careful to make the verb agree in number with its antecedent (the word it refers to). The entire meaning of the sentence may hinge on the verb choice.

Our contract includes a *clause* with several mistakes *that is* meant to confuse the buyer. (The entire clause is meant to confuse the buyer.)

Our contract includes a clause with several *mistakes that are* meant to confuse the buyer. (The mistakes, rather than the entire clause, are meant to confuse the buyer.)

THERAPY 7

Correct the subject-verb agreement errors in the following sentences. Write "correct" in the margin beside each statement without errors. Underline all simple subjects and verbs.

1. The <u>number</u> of attachments included with these forms ~~are~~ <u>exceeded</u> only by the number of attachments enclosed with the last form <u>we</u> <u>sent</u> you.
   is

2. The array of educational programs benefit both the students and the company.

3. Inside this old file cabinet are a collector's item commonly known as the pencil.

4. The deficiency in math and science skills among the top executives point to major problems of productivity.

5. Want ads say that all job categories from receptionist to undertaker require a high level of mathematical skills.

6. Shuffling added, amended, qualified, and initialed paragraphs certainly make a contract look negotiable.

7. We have been told that the equipment at all branches need repairs.

8. Three hours is a long time to be in the air, particularly without a parachute.

9. Neither lack of money nor lack of praise keep John from coming to the office each day.

10. He outlined all the errors in our reasoning that has caused us continuing problems.

11. Each manager, along with all the sales people in the territory, are eligible to attend the seminar.

12. In defense of everything I said yesterday during the meeting is the signed contracts.

13. We have not talked with a single one of the instructors who have complained about having you in our seminar.

14. All of the painting including the other maintenance work have been completed.

15. He has a file containing several of our complaints, which need daily updating.

16. My interest is primarily stocks and bonds.

8

AGREEMENT—VIEWPOINT, VOICE, TENSES, MOOD

Viewpoints, voices, moods, and tenses do not always have to agree from sentence to sentence, but there generally should be agreement within clauses. Unnecessary viewpoint, voice, mood, or tense changes often create ambiguity. Let's get specific.

VIEWPOINT

Viewpoint—mine, yours, the other person's?

A *first-person* viewpoint means that you are referring to yourself as writer (*I, me*) or to yourself and at least one other person (*we, us*). A *second-person* viewpoint means that you are talking directly *to* one or more people (*you*). A *third-person* viewpoint means that you are talking *about* people, things, or ideas (*he, they, one, problems*).

First person: I can get in the building with the right credentials.

Second person:	You can get inside the building with whatever credentials you can forge.
Third person:	Mark Spitauli can get in the building with only a smile and a wink.

Some changes in viewpoint are fine. During the course of a long narrative such as this book, I have changed viewpoint, voice, mood, and tense many times. So will you in business writing.

For example, in a letter to a client you may say, *"I was* glad to talk with you on the phone last Friday and to assure you that *we will provide* the services *you need.* Please *call* me if *you have* questions about what the *vendor included* on the billing."

But be careful about unnecessary changes.

Inappropriate change:	All vendors should send their invoices directly to us, and you should also include your employer identification number.
Restructured: (Second person)	You should send your invoices directly to us, and you should also include your employer identification number.
Restructured: (Third person)	All vendors should send their invoices directly to us, and they should also include their employer identification number.

VOICE

No, you do not "hear" voices. Nevertheless, verbs are said to have voice. With *active-voice* verbs, the subject acts. With *passive-voice* verbs, the subject does nothing; it sits passively and receives the action of the verb.

Passive: Our company's dress code *was established* by a nun living in the fourteenth century.
Active: A nun living in the fourteenth century *established* our company's dress code.

Passive: The reports *are designed* to improve your rating with the boss.
Active: We *design* the reports to improve your rating with the boss.

Passive: These tools *should be used* only in case of emergency, such as a headache.
Active: You *should use* these tools only in case of an emergency, such as a headache.

Passive: The proposal that you get twelve weeks' vacation each year actually *has been approved* by the CEO.
Active: The CEO *has approved* the proposal that you get twelve weeks' vacation each year.

Passive: Our analyst *was injured* by a man-eating computer.
Active: A man-eating computer *injured* our analyst.

Don't carelessly switch voice within a clause or sentence:

Unnecessary Change: The *proposals were sealed* by the bidders, but upon learning of the budget increase, *they rebid* the jobs with great eagerness.
Restructured: The *bidders had sealed* their proposals, but upon learning of the budget increase, *they rebid* the jobs with great eagerness.

Unnecessary   Sales *plummeted* and *were expected*
Change: to do so.
Restructured: *We expected* sales to plummet, and
                    they did.
Restructured: *Sales plummeted* as *we expected.*

You'll notice that active-voice verbs sound stronger and command more attention than passive-voice verbs. Passive-voice verbs exemplify their name; they seem limp, lazy, and lifeless. Passive-voice verbs, however, can help you hedge your message by hiding "doers" in sentences, and passive-voice verbs can add courtesy by softening commands.

> The decision to fire twenty people has already been made. (You want to cover up or downplay who made the decision.)
>
> A mistake was made in transferring the funds. (You don't want to accept responsibility yourself!)
>
> These forms should be sent to my office by noon. (You don't want to sound too demanding with a direct active-voice command: Send these forms to my office by noon.)

To be clear, direct, and emphatic in your writing, prefer active-voice verbs.

TENSES

You do not need to memorize the various tenses because most native English speakers choose the appropriate verb tense without much thought. However, do review the examples that follow so that you will notice unnecessary changes that create ambiguity in your own writing.

Simple Active Voice

Present:	I *deserve* attention today.
Past:	I *deserved* attention yesterday.
Future:	I *will deserve* attention next week.
Present Perfect:	I *have deserved* all the attention bestowed upon me during my lifetime.
Past Perfect:	I *had deserved* all the attention given to me prior to the unsatisfactory report; I don't understand why the attention stopped.
Future Perfect:	I *will have deserved* all of the attention this proposal brings me when I submit it next week.

Progressive Active Voice (action in progress)

Present:	I *am working* today.
Past:	I *was working* when you called earlier this morning.
Future:	I *will be working* all day.
Present Perfect:	I *have been working* all day.
Past Perfect:	I *had been working* two hours before the siren sounded.
Future Perfect:	I *will have been working* here six months before I receive the first promised raise.

Simple Passive Voice

Present:	The information *is presented* on film.
Past:	The information *was presented* on film last week.
Future:	The information *will be presented* on film for the next six weeks.
Present Perfect:	The information *had been pre-*

	sented on film before he even made his request for the showing.
Future Perfect:	The information *will have been presented* on film to all employees before they assume their positions on August 2.

Some tenses, of course, will not agree from clause to clause or sentence to sentence. If you are talking about different time frames, you must, of course, mix tenses.

After studying the report, we *have concluded* that it *is* best to decline the offer. By December 31, we *will have lost* $2 million, and we *can't hope* to have enough cash on hand to purchase the equipment he *is offering*. We *wish* we *had known* of his offer earlier in the year.

Kelly *said* he *thinks* the position *is* still open.

Kelly *says* he *thought* the position *was* still open when he *talked* to her last week.

The manager *insists* that she *has seen* your portfolio and that she *will be evaluating* it next week.

The manager *insisted* that she *had seen* your portfolio and that she *will ignore* your application when you *arrive* for the interview.

Don't, however, switch tenses unnecessarily.

There *appears* to be a variation in the expenses reported by sales people attending the convention. Don Brown's report *shows* a hotel charge of $482. Margaret White's report *lists* charges of $628. Bob Attaboy's report *indicated* an expenditure of $842. (You noted the tense change to *indicated*—past tense. Was Bob Attaboy's report submitted for a trip taken earlier than the other two? If Bob submitted his report at the same time, there's no reason for the tense change.)

Unnecessary tense changes always raise questions.

NOTE: Regardless of other verb tenses in a sentence, you should express a subordinate-clause verb in the present tense if it expresses a general principle.

The Supreme Court *ruled* that companies such as ours *are* not responsible for damages of this nature.

MOOD

Sentences can be written in three moods. No, I don't mean the writer can be in one of three moods; the sentence itself expresses a mood: *indicative* mood, *imperative* mood, or *subjunctive* mood.

Indicative Mood

Indicative-mood sentences state a fact or ask a question.

Do you constantly run out of time while your boss runs out of work?

Most time-consuming tasks on your desk are the result of other people's problems.

I can tell you how I grapple with office politics: I play along.

Imperative Mood

Imperative-mood sentences give commands.

Return the enclosed card today for your one-in-400 million chance to make $10.

Blithersmith, analyze just what it is that makes you such a grouch every morning when you come to work.

Delegate this work to your boss.

Subjunctive Mood

Subjunctive-mood sentences state conditions that are contrary to fact (or highly unlikely), express doubt, state strong wishes or demands, make concessions, show necessity, or show resolution.

To show subjunctive mood, reverse everything you've learned so far. (Almost.) That is, use a plural verb with a singular subject. To express present time, use the past tense. To express past time, use the present tense. With all forms of *to be* verbs, show the subjunctive mood with the single word *be*.

If lack of skill *were* the problem, I would give you a book to solve all your headaches. (Lack of skill isn't the problem.)

If he *were* a millionaire, he would take this job and give it to someone else. (He's not a millionaire.)

If I *were* you, I'd turn this problem over to my secretary and take a vacation until things calm down. (I am not you.)

I demand that he *leave* the branch office immediately. (The indicative-mood verb is *he leaves,* but the clause expresses a demand, not a fact.)

That he *trust* the lawyer is essential. (Indicative-mood sentence: That he *trusts* the lawyer is a given.) This subjunctive-mood sentence expresses a necessity, not a fact.

I suggest that she *be reinstated* immediately. (Indicative-mood sentence: She *is reinstated*.) This subjunctive-mood sentence expresses a wish, not a fact.

RESOLVED: That Helen Harkens *be issued* a $200 fine. (Indicative-mood sentence: *Helen is issued* a $200 fine.) This subjunctive-mood sentence states a resolution.

We agreed that he *be hired* for that job. (Indicative-mood sentence: He *is hired*.) This subjunctive-mood sentence shows concession.

We let nothing *detract* us from our card game at lunch. (Indicative-mood sentence: Nothing *detracts* us from our card game at lunch.) This subjunctive-mood sentence expresses resolution or strong wish.

If I *take* this job, I *will expect* a raise. (Indicative-mood sentence: Probable—I may take it.)

If I *took* this job, I *would expect* a raise. (Subjunctive-mood sentence: Highly unlikely—I probably won't take it.)

MAJOR RELAPSES

The most common viewpoint, voice, mood, and tense switches seem to occur in procedure or instructional writing. And, more often than not, such changes create ambiguity. Of course, you cannot and should not always use the same viewpoint or tense from sentence to sentence. If you are speaking both to or about people, you need to change viewpoints. If you are talking about two different time periods, you need to change tenses. But take care with such changes and know why you are switching from present to past tense or from the indicative to the subjunctive mood. Careless changes usually raise questions in the reader's mind.

THERAPY 8

Correct the unnecessary viewpoint, voice, mood, or tense changes in the following sentences.

1. I am planning a retirement luncheon for Taylor Toyauski, and I ~~would~~ recommend that the luncheon ~~is~~ be held before he ~~left~~ leaves the company.

2. We have confirmed reservations in your name, and your room charges have been prepaid by us also.

3. We have compiled *Manpower and the Monkey* to give you the necessary information, and it was edited and updated as we have experienced a quantum leap of energy.

4. Managers should comment on writing skills in performance appraisals, and you should also recommend self-study texts for improvements.

5. All of the expenses that go on the forms for reimbursement should be approved by department heads

or their designated representatives. Please review
these for accuracy.

6. This system makes it easy for you to boost payments on long standing accounts. Users will also
have an invaluable checklist of ten ways to spot a
company in financial trouble.

7. This situation seems to have slipped out of hand,
and I would suggest that we call in a consultant
immediately to see if we can dismiss the whole
crew and start over.

8. The instructor must provide a recommended reading list by August; the tuition will be paid in full by
September.

9. Please sign here, and you should also pay me now.

10. The managers gathered at his retirement dinner,
and great eagerness to say goodbye was expressed.

9

PUNCTUATION

Punctuation makes writing readable. You may have run across this little ditty somewhere:

What is is what is not is not is it not

This nonsensical statement really does have meaning when you add the punctuation marks:

What is, is; what is not, is not; is it not?

Learn to think of punctuation marks as road signs to simplify, not complicate, writing. Most marks are a matter of common sense and clarity.

Punctuation rules, however, are continually evolving with our language. And some punctuation marks depend on voice inflection and emphasis. For example, one writer might pause where the commas are in the following sentence; another writer might not pause at all:

We told him about the job, and we, [pause] therefore, [pause] fully expect him to accept it.

We told him about the job, and we therefore fully expect him to accept it.

In other words, the writer who pauses before and after *therefore* considers the word an "interrupter" to the smooth flow of the sentence and thus sets *therefore* off with commas. The writer who reads this sentence with no pause may consider *therefore* to be a vital part of the last clause and may not use commas around it.

Most punctuation principles, however, are *not* subject to interpretation like the one above. Therefore, you need to learn the following punctuation guides as a matter of correctness and clarity. When you come to optional rules (or principles), you'll find notes about the exceptions.

COMMAS

To Introduce

Think of the introductory comma as a means to help the reader quickly skim over the less-important words, phrases, or clauses and focus on the main idea of the sentence.

Use a comma after introductory words.

Actually, I would work at this job even if they didn't pay me.

Frankly, I can think of easier ways to make a living.

Zelda, what would I have to do to get you to forward money by the end of the week to pay my airfare home? (Sets off noun of direct address)

Wait, let me assure you that I am responsible for absolutely nothing in this office.

Use a comma after an introductory verbal or elliptical phrase.

> When asking your subordinates to do "exception" reporting, make sure you define the exception.

> After transcribing his correspondence, she knows enough to keep the grapevine busy for the next two months.

> To get an answer, I think you're going to have to broaden the question.

> Considering the way you bungled this project, I suggest that you have someone sample your food from the company cafeteria.

Use a comma after two or more long introductory prepositional phrases.

> At the beginning of the Hitton project, we had a clear understanding of our goals; now we have no idea what they were.

> In all cases of gross neglect of the security measures, the auditors noted missing equipment.

Use a comma after an introductory adverbial clause.

> If you have questions, please hesitate before calling me.

> As working conditions improve, salaries decrease.

> I know that you have worked here a long time, but *when all your friends leave the company,* your job is ripe for a takeover move.

NOTE: In the last sentence the *when your friends leave the company* clause is not introductory to the entire sentence, but it introduces the main clause in the last half of the sentence. The comma before *but* in the last example is a comma that separates—something we'll get to later.

NOTE: If you reverse the placement of the two clauses in the previous examples (with the adverbial clause coming at the end), the sentences do not require an introductory comma.

Salaries decrease as working conditions improve.

Please hesitate before calling me if you have questions.

Major Relapses

If you carelessly omit an introductory comma, you may cause misreading or create an unintentional fragment.

Fragment:	For whatever reason the meeting was postponed.
Sentence:	For whatever reason, the meeting was postponed.
Unclear:	After welding this pipe must be buried.
Clear:	After welding, this pipe must be buried.

Remember that the reader does not have your voice inflection to know when to pause. You must write in the pause with a comma.

To Separate

Use a comma to separate main clauses joined by a coordinate conjunction (*and, but, for, nor, or, so, yet*). A main clause, you remember, expresses a complete thought and can stand alone.

I have prepared this stupid report, and you're going to read every last word of it.

He gets confused looking at statistics, so he has arranged to explain this concept with fiddlesticks to the board of directors.

I wouldn't say my secretary is slow getting back to callers, but occasionally she puts them on hold and goes out to lunch.

NOTE: You may omit the comma if the main clauses are very short.

I entered the room and he exited.

NOTE: Do not use a comma to separate clauses joined by *so that*; *so that* is a subordinate, not coordinate, conjunction. That is, *so that* subordinates the clause that follows rather than links it equally to the previous idea.

I need your help so that I have someone to blame if the project backfires.

Use a comma to separate items in a series.

The frown on the customer's face may mean that he dislikes you, hates the product, or has hemorrhoids.

This course was written for researchers, personnel specialists, and managers.

NOTE: The comma before the *and* in the previous sentence is optional. However, the trend is to include this last comma in a series because, without it, the last two items may occasionally appear to be a single unit. For example, in the previous sentence, without the comma *personnel specialists* and *managers* may refer to the same group of people. With the comma the sentence clearly refers to three different groups.

Use a comma to separate two or more adjectives modifying the same noun when the *and* is omitted.

From her telephone voice, David imagined her to be a dim-witted, unreasonable negotiator.

This situation will ultimately demand a lengthy, expensive lawsuit.

NOTE: Do not use a comma between two or more adjectives if they do not equally modify the noun that follows.

He designed a snazzy new four-color brochure for the product. (You would not say "a snazzy and new and four-color brochure." Therefore, commas between the adjectives in sentences such as this are incorrect.)

Major Relapses

Do not use a comma simply to separate subject from verb. Many writers have a habit of putting in a comma wherever they breathe. Therefore, if the complete subject is a long one, they tend to take a breath and, thus, write a comma between the subject and verb. Commas used to separate must separate main clauses, items in a series, or two adjectives modifying the same noun equally.

Incorrect:	Outlining important ideas and practical recommendations for more effective staffing, is his only area of expertise.
Correct:	Outlining important ideas and practical recommendations for more effective staffing is his only area of expertise.

Also, be sure that the comma does not simply separate a compound verb rather than two complete clauses.

Incorrect: The supervisor looked into the solution, and found no problem.

Correct: The supervisor looked into the solution and found no problem.

Correct: The supervisor looked into the solution, and *she* found no problem. (We've added a subject and now have two clauses.)

To Enclose

Use commas to cut away nonessential (or interrupting) words and phrases from the rest of the sentence. Some of the most common interrupting phrases are these: *for instance, to be sure, on the other hand, on the contrary.*

The weather, at least according to my thermometer, may prohibit further testing today.

He has a one-track mind and, consequently, has difficulty talking and thinking at the same time.

The maintenance crew around here is, theoretically at least, acquainted with the products we sell.

We think you'll agree, for the most part, that your skills became obsolete right after World War I.

He looks to be of Spanish descent, but his name, to be sure, is Irish.

These commas to restrict (or set off) are particularly important with modifying participial phrases.

John showed us the letter pinpointing the morale problem. (The letter pinpointed the morale problem.)

John showed us the letter, pinpointing the morale problem. (The comma cuts the phrase away from *letter*. John pinpointed the morale problem.)

Better: Pinpointing the morale problem, John showed us the letter. (The participial phrase is now introductory and is closer to *John*, the word it modifies.)

Also, use commas to cut away nonessential *clauses* from the rest of the sentence.

Think of commas to enclose as parentheses. When you enclose a clause, phrase, or word inside commas, you are indicating that the reader can omit the part set off by commas without changing the meaning of the words that are left.

Essential:	I saw the man who left in the Porsche. (Tells which specific man)
Nonessential:	I saw the man, who left in the Porsche. (The reader knows which man. The "who" clause simply adds information about how the man left.)
Essential:	The mayor exited as though she'd been shot out of a cannon. (Essential to tell how she exited)
Nonessential:	The mayor sauntered to the meeting, as though time were of no importance. (Adds an afterthought)
Essential:	I mailed the letter before he called me about the invoice. (Essential to tell when the letter was mailed)
Nonessential:	I mailed the letter Wednesday, before he called about the invoice. (Adds further explanation about when the letter was mailed)
Essential:	My approval is necessary unless the customer has proper identification.

	(Gives an essential exception to the necessary approval)
Nonessential:	My approval is necessary, unless you want to take the responsibility for the damage yourself. (Adds an afterthought)
Essential:	My colleague whom I consider the least knowledgeable on the subject agrees that we made the right decision. (Tells which specific colleague)
Nonessential:	My colleague, whom I consider the least knowledgeable on the subject, agrees that we've made the right decision. (Does not distinguish one colleague from another; simply adds unnecessary information about the colleague)

Try this test when writing: Put commas around the questionable clause, and then read the sentence eliminating that part. If what's left doesn't make sense or if the meaning of the remaining words changes, don't use commas around the clause in question.

Bill is one of the few people I know, who has a doctorate in psychology.

Is this comma correct or not? Let's try the test. Omit the part after the comma and read what remains: *Bill is one of the few people I know.* Is that the meaning of the sentence? No, the writer means that Bill is one of the few people among his acquaintances with a doctorate in psychology. Therefore, don't use a comma to cut away that information from the rest of the sentence; the *who* clause is essential to qualify the meaning of *one*.

On the other hand, try this sentence:

The pink packing slip, which I intend to enclose in the package, has three items listed.

Leave out the part between the commas and see if this is the true meaning: *The pink packing slip has three items listed*. Yes, that clause makes sense alone; the omission of the words *which I intend to enclose in the package* doesn't change the meaning of what remains. The enclosed *which* clause simply adds information; therefore, this clause is correctly enclosed with commas.

Try another example. Remember, commas to set off or enclose a clause indicate that the clause *adds* nonessential information. Do not set off or enclose a clause that is essential to *restrict or qualify* the meaning of the other words in the sentence.

He doesn't like to answer questions that show his lack of expertise on the subject (The *that* clause is not set off with commas because *that show his lack of expertise on the subject* qualifies or restricts *questions;* he doesn't like to answer specific questions that show lack of expertise, but he may like to answer easy questions.)

My friend, who speaks no English, has been hired to answer the phones. (We know which friend. With commas around the *who* clause, the writer is simply adding the fact the friend speaks no English.)

My friend who speaks no English has been hired to answer the phones. (Without commas round the *who* clause, the writer tells *which* friend was hired—the friend who speaks no English as opposed to the friend with a master's degree in English.)

Remember that the comma says to the reader, "Stop reading—end of idea." When no comma stops the reader, the information qualifies the nearby word or phrase.

Major Relapses

Remember that commas to enclose come in pairs like a set of parentheses.

Incorrect:	My boss, Joe Dotz from Minneapolis has decided to give everyone a Christmas bonus this year: 50 cents.
Correct:	My boss, Joe Dotz from Minneapolis, has decided to give everyone a Christmas bonus this year: 50 cents.
Incorrect:	He has created problems with most, if not all of our clients by brushing his teeth in his water glass at the lunch table.
Correct:	He has created problems with most, if not all, of our clients by brushing his teeth in his water glass at the lunch table.
Incorrect:	The mortician who spoke immediately before the awards banquet, created tension about the reason for unspecified bonuses.
Correct:	The mortician, who spoke immediately before the awards banquet, created tension about the reason for unspecified bonuses.

To Add or Contradict

Use a comma to tag on an additional thought at the end of a sentence or to contradict the first thought.

The company does not insist that you transfer to Alaska, only that you arrange to pick up your paycheck there each week.

That was the correct solution, wasn't it?

You can call me with problems day or night at home or at the office, if calling toll-free.

She approves millions of dollars for equipment, but nothing for employee bonuses.

All Other Miscellaneous Commas

The first four kinds of commas (to introduce, to separate, to enclose, and to add or contradict) are the ones that give people the most problems. Other miscellaneous uses for the comma follow:

After salutations	Dear Fred,
After closings	Sincerely,
Within dates	I accepted the job October 15, 1982, and resigned October 16, 1986. (You may omit the comma after the year.)
To separate elements in an address	Please forward all money to 100 Million Street, Moneytown, Texas, in order that I may take the next plane to Acapulco. (You may omit the comma after *Texas*.)
Between a name and degree	Joan Daviddingler, Ph.D.
Between a name and title	Robert Comquat, Vice President of Marketing
To show omission of words	I contributed 90 percent of the effort; John, 10 percent.
To prevent mis-reading	I don't know if this is the correct timing; that is is the product ready for market now? *Clear:* I don't know if

this is the correct timing;
that is, is the product ready
for market now?

NOTE: For comma placement with quotes, parentheses, brackets, or dashes, see those headings.

SEMICOLONS

Missing Conjunctions

Semicolons take the place of missing coordinate conjunctions (*and, but, or, nor, for, so, yet*).

She makes a strong case in her letter threatening legal action; perhaps I should swallow my pride while it will still go down without too much pain.

You may argue that our standards of recruitment are high; we require a 5.0 grade-point average.

A wise manager looks well to the waists of his employees; obesity, heart attack, and high blood pressure are expensive to subsidize.

You can also separate the ideas in the preceding examples into two sentences. The semicolon simply shows a closer relationship between ideas than a period does.

Before Connective Adverbs

Semicolons precede connective adverbs such as *consequently, furthermore, hence, however, thus, moreover, nevertheless, otherwise, still, therefore, then, accordingly.*

The machinists at five aerospace companies are being given a sixteen-week course on how to operate our new computers; however, the computers will be outdated in about two months.

This job is dangerous; therefore, we have purchased a couple of ambulances for daily use.

I don't want to imply that the assignment is politically motivated; nevertheless, I advise you not to leave the meeting early.

As a Comma "Upgrade"

You've heard of upgrading your computer system? Think of the semicolon as a way to upgrade a comma; a semicolon can bring your reader to a fuller stop than a comma. If phrases, clauses, or single-word items in a series already have internal commas, you may use semicolons to "upgrade" the commas that represent the biggest breaks.

He has given us basic guidelines on performance appraisals, along with schedules; management development, including succession of key personnel; compensation cost; and personnel planning.

We have hired a PR firm, Bullet and Morris Inc., to help us to intensify internal competition, which has not yet developed among the departments; but we plan to audit the PR firm's results daily. (Because the first half of the sentence has several internal commas, the semicolon between the two main clauses helps the reader more quickly visualize the two most important ideas given in the main clauses.)

Major Relapses

The major problems with the use of the semicolon are unintentional run-on sentences and comma splices:

Incorrect: He did not like the situation developing in the branch office, however, he felt he had no authority to correct it.

Incorrect: You could be cured of the seven-year itch while waiting for his approval on

the expenditures, therefore, I suggest
that you don't ask.

These examples have two complete sentences jammed
together. A comma in front of the *however* and *therefore* is
not strong enough to hold these clauses apart. In the ab-
sence of a coordinate conjunction (*and, but, or, for, nor,
so, yet*), you must have a semicolon before a connective
adverb such as *however, moreover, thus, therefore*. Or you
must break the information into two sentences with a period.

Correct: He did not like the situation developing
             in the branch office; however, he felt he
             had no authority to correct it.
Correct: You could be cured of the seven-year
             itch while waiting for his approval on
             the expenditures. Therefore, I suggest
             that you don't ask.

NOTE: Watch for these adverbs used simply as transition
words:

Correct: Before you invest in too many uniforms,
             therefore, I suggest you take another
             look at the work schedule and the cafe-
             teria food. (The *therefore* in this exam-
             ple is a transition word referring to an
             earlier idea. The commas before and
             after *therefore* are correct here because
             the part of the sentence preceding *there-
             fore* cannot stand alone. *Before you in-
             vest in too many uniforms* is an
             introductory subordinate clause, not a
             main clause giving a complete thought.)

COLONS

Use a colon when a word, phrase, or clause amplifies or further explains the first part of the sentence. The colon stresses, or highlights, what follows.

My secretary is a jujitsu expert: she keeps people out of my hair and off my back.

He has two dictation speeds: fast forward and rewind.

I think the error can be traced to only one cause: stupidity.

Use a colon to introduce a series.

The president has four criteria for hiring engineers: a college education, two years' experience, a positive attitude, and no concern about salary.

NOTE: Do *not* use a colon to introduce a series of items, people, or ideas that are direct objects of the verb or are objects of a preposition. (Exception: You may use a colon in this way before a formal list beginning on a succeeding line.)

Incorrect:	We shipped several items, including: a typewriter, a CPU, and a sledgehammer.
Correct:	We shipped several items, including a typewriter, a CPU, and a sledgehammer.
Incorrect:	They have: permission to negotiate, time to delay, authority to lie, and money to waste.
Correct:	They have permission to negotiate, time to delay, authority to lie, and money to waste.

Correct: They have:
              1) permisson to negotiate
              2) time to delay
              3) authority to lie
              4) money to waste

Other Miscellaneous Uses for a Colon

To introduce a long or formal quotation

Correct: The Booher principle is this: The chance of an almost-right word creeping into a report is directly proportional to the executive rank of the reader.

NOTE: Capitalize the first word of a main clause after the colon only when it demands special emphasis because it is a formal principle, quote, or saying.

To follow a salutation

Dear Sir or Madam:

To separate parts of bibliographic entries and titles, biblical references, and clock times

John 3:16

6:45 a.m.

Would You Put That in Writing: How to Write Your Way to Success in Business, New York: Facts On File, Inc., 1983. (Just a little free advertising here.)

CONFUSION ABOUT SEMICOLONS, COLONS, AND PERIODS

Despite all the foregoing guidelines, some writers still find choices between a period and a semicolon or between a semicolon and a colon difficult. The difference is particularly confusing when the choice is a matter of interpretation. Consider these further guides:

- A period shows less connection between two ideas than a semicolon does.
- Semicolons emphasize all main clauses in a sentence equally.
- Colons emphasize the second thought in the sentence more than the first thought.

This is the situation: his performance problem will not go away; we're going to have to dismiss him. (The colon is used to emphasize what follows it. The last two thoughts explain the opening clause. The last two clauses are joined by a semicolon rather than a period because they are very closely related.)

These same ideas can be correctly written as separate sentences. But the connection between thoughts is vague, and the sentences sound choppy and disjointed.

This is the situation. His performance problem will not go away. We're going to have to dismiss him.

PERIODS

Use periods to end statements, even when a statement implies a question.

After my stint in Personnel, I am wondering if more and more people are using resumes to fabricate a past and to create a future.

Use periods with commands and with questions intended as softened commands.

Do not interrupt me again.

Turn off the electricity on his research project.

Would you please include the price of each item in your letter.

Miscellaneous Uses for Periods

To form some abbreviations

i.e.   Mrs.   2 p.m.
(But: IBM, UCLA, OPEC)

To follow numbers in lists or outlines

I.
  A.
    1.
    2.

To separate whole numbers from decimals

526.22   43.6 percent

To set off run-in headings

Pricing. Prices have fluctuated . . .

NOTE: For placement of periods with quotation marks, parentheses, and brackets, see those headings.

QUESTION MARKS

Writers seldom have problems with question marks. Occasional indecision arises about indirect questions and about commands disguised as questions.

Use a question mark after a *direct* question but not after an *indirect* question.

He asked if I understood the difference between a merit raise and a bribe. (Indirect question)

He asked, "Do you understand the difference between a merit raise and a bribe?" (Direct question)

Meryl asked how to sort the prospects for the sales force. (Indirect question)

Meryl asked, "How do I sort the prospects for the sales force?" (Direct question)

As a lawyer, I frequently get this question: Do I owe you if we lose? (Direct question)

My response is usually, Do you want me to prepare before we go to court? (Direct question)

Use a period with a softened command; use a question mark with a true request.

Would you please forward all of the computer printouts to me by Friday. (The writer expects the reader to forward the printouts.)

Can you forward all of the computer printouts to me by Friday? (The writer is really asking if this is a possibility, not commanding.)

QUOTATION MARKS

Use quotation marks around the exact words of a speaker but not around paraphrases of the exact words.

Would you excuse me to phone my manager to tell her that you're not nearly the incompetent jerk she said you were? (Paraphrase)

My manager said, "Rupert is an incompetent employee." (Exact quotation)

I began to wonder if my age were a problem when my boss wrote "needs refurbishing" on my performance appraisal. ("Needs refurbishing" is an exact quotation.)

NOTE: If a long quotation is to be set in contrasting typescript or indented with wider margins than the rest of the text, do not use quotation marks.

We can safely assume consultant Harry Jones does not advocate the commonly accepted tendencies. He writes convincingly:

The maternalistic secretary is motivated by her need to dominate, master, and control combined with an equally deep need to gain the love, affection, and appreciation of those whom she tortures.

If the long quotation is set in the same typescript and with the same margins as the rest of the text, use quotation marks at the beginning of the quoted material, at the beginning of each new paragraph, and then at the end of the last paragraph.

Martin Glower offered the following observations about his colleague: "In managing an office system, she seeks to avoid pressuring people, so she does not ask for increased productivity.

"If her employees make dentist appointments at ten in the morning, she grins and bears the burden alone.

"If they call in sick, she suggests back rubs. If they have fever, she pops chicken soup in the microwave for home delivery.

"Whatever the situation, we can safely assume that she hears all opinions and ideas and accepts all radical behavior with a blank stare and a stoic attitude. In our last stress-reduction seminar, she registered ten on a scale of one to five."

Use single quotation marks when you enclose a direct quotation within a quotation.

His letter stipulates the following detail: "The bid 'however designed' must be in my office by Friday, May 6."

NOTE: Computer languages often require single quotation marks as part of programming. Don't confuse their use in such languages with normal English usage.

Use quotation marks to enclose misnomers, coined words, or slang terms that do not match the tone of the rest of the sentence. However, be careful not to overuse quotation marks for such reasons because they lose their impact in calling attention to unusual wording.

Thank the telephone operator for her "help" in putting the call through to London. (Meaning the operator was no help at all)

The caller seemed to be a drugged "flake" rather than someone with malicious intent to cause harm to our board members.

Use quotation marks to enclose titles of poems, stories, chapters, papers, or articles appearing in a larger work.

"Molecular Noise" was part of the collected papers presented at the February symposium, and we have reprinted it in our new book *Biochemistry in Our Decade*.

Rules about quotation marks used in conjunction with commas and periods often bring resistance because they are illogical rules. Never mind, just learn them.

Place commas and periods *inside* closing quotation marks—regardless of meaning.

> If the document stipulates "damaged merchandise," turn the claim over to our insurance company.

> The autocratic boss says, "My people work *for* me, not *with* me."

Place semicolons and colons *outside* closing quotation marks—regardless of meaning.

> Our service technician insists that he "did not damage the roof of the customer's garage"; however, he does admit that the falling roof damaged him.

> The window washers in our building earn more than "a pittance": $42 an hour.

Place question marks and exclamation points *inside or outside* closing quotation marks—depending on meaning.

> Why is the report for the vice president always found in the last file drawer marked "active"?

> I know I'm going to work late when my boss asks, "Have you seen that file I had on my desk yesterday?"

> As he collapsed with a heart attack, he shouted, "We made quota!"

> Think of the "rewards"!

NOTE: Congressional records and some legal documents have commas and periods both inside and outside closing quotation marks for exactness reasons. The British system of punctuation is another exception to the preceding rule about placement of periods and commas within closing quotation marks. With the British system, periods and commas can go on either side of the closing quotation marks, according to the sentence meaning.

ELLIPSES

Ellipses represent pauses in dialogue or words omitted within quoted material.

Use three dots to show the omission of words in the middle of a sentence. Use four dots to show the omission of words at the end of a sentence. (Three dots show the omission of words, and the fourth dot signifies the period at the end of the sentence.)

The pamphlet says, "The instructor will determine the number of attendees admitted to the class . . . and will decide whether attendees should receive credit for the course."

The pamphlet says, "The instructor will determine the number of attendees admitted to the class. . . ."

If the quoted material is clearly only part of a sentence, an ellipsis is unnecessary and incorrect. But if the quoted material appears to be a complete sentence, use an ellipsis to show the quoted material had either preceding or following words.

I can assure you that the contract "will be given full consideration." (Clearly only part of the text)

". . . The matter is closed," he assured us in his letter.

Use an ellipsis to indicate a pause in spoken dialogue.

He said, "I think . . . no, I know who sounded the alarm."

DASHES

Dashes, less formal than colons, emphasize the word, phrase, or clause set off from the rest of the sentence. They are typed as two hyphens.

Joan Dimwit has three major interests on the job--money, management, and men.

Martin Martyr had a good reason for resigning--he had been stealing from the company.

Use a dash to set off words that explain a preceding series.

Zack from Accounting, Gertrude from Sales, Billy Bob from Data Processing—these are the people who get things done despite setbacks.

Use a dash to add effect or create suspense.

The boss treats us all the same—as slaves.

He who laughs last—may get fired.

Use dashes instead of commas to set off modifiers and appositives when commas may cause misreading.

Unclear:	The retired employee embarrassed his mother, a sanitation supervisor, and himself on the steps of corporate headquarters. (He embarrassed two people or three?)
Clear:	The retired employee embarrassed his mother—a sanitation supervisor—and

himself on the steps of corporate headquarters.

If the context calls for a dash where a comma would
ordinarily be inserted, omit the comma.

If he phones—and I don't expect him to—tell him I'll
be in Malaysia for the next three years; I'll return his
call when I get back.

If the parenthetical element requires a question mark or
exclamation point, use it.

The board members adjourned—did you know about
the meeting?—before taking final action.

PARENTHESES

Words, phrases, or clauses set off with parentheses
show less relationship to the rest of the sentence than those
set off by commas or dashes. In other words, dashes and
colons emphasize whereas parentheses subordinate.

He invited several managers—Ted Crum, Lisa Politely,
Hank Ripover—to the press conference. (Emphasizes
the names. These people are bigwigs in the company.)

He invited several managers (Ted Crum, Lisa Politely,
Hank Ripover) to the press conference. (Subordinates
the names. Most readers will probably not care who the
specific managers were.)

Parentheses set off parenthetical thoughts—ideas not
essential to the meaning of the sentence or the paragraph.

We have supplied all the information about the customers that we could possibly discover (everything but weight and sexual preference).

Parentheses also enclose numbers, acronyms, or abbreviations. With acronyms and the exact terms they stand for, enclose the less-familiar term.

OPEC (Organization of Petroleum Exporting Countries) gave us a deadline for this response.

Operators must be familiar with all functions, particularly the Get Next (GN) command.

The audit report was not exactly comprehensive in that it (1) identified no bogus bonuses, (2) verified compliance with only two contracts, and (3) recommended no policies to prevent future problems.

If the parentheses enclose a complete sentence within a paragraph, place the period inside the parentheses.

We were unable to discover all the information the vice president requested. (We did include shoe size and marital status.) All the information we did collect has been sent to her by overnight express.

If the parentheses enclose a complete sentence that interrupts the main clause of another sentence, do not use a period unless the parenthetical element requires a different mark than the sentence as a whole.

How we developed a system of payments that contradicts society's work ethics (we ourselves have never approved of the concept of unemployment benefits) illustrates exactly how difficult controlling a government can be.

We need to send another copy of the letter (should we include the invoice too?) before he calls a second time.

If the parentheses contain a *short* sentence, you may or may not want to interrupt the flow of the main sentence. You have two choices:

Marital status of the barmaids is given later in the report (see Table 2).

Marital status of the barmaids is given later in the report. (See Table 2.)

When the closing parenthesis comes where you would ordinarily use a comma, place the comma after the parenthetical information.

Our materials for the supervisory skills seminar included case studies (developed by the participants themselves), a videotape series, and workbooks.

BRACKETS

Use brackets to set off sections that are already enclosed in parentheses.

(During the past ten years, the author has also conducted practical research [see tabulations on the next page] to identify key hiring philosophies and issues.)

Brackets also indicate the writer's addition to quoted words when the direct quote is incomplete and needs explanation.

"I don't like it [the bulldozer approach], but I use it because that's the corporate culture here." (The writer has defined the *it,* which was perhaps clear in the entire context, but unclear from the excerpt the writer has chosen to use.)

PUNCTUATING A FORMAL LIST

When punctuating a formal list, you have several options. You may either add punctuation after each item in the list or omit punctuation altogether, letting the layout of the list guide the reader's eye from item to item. Items in a list that are complete sentences themselves, however, do require end punctuation.

Correct   We have three choices:
- Transfer to another division
- Resignation from the committee
- Jail

Correct: The contract stipulates:
(1) Barko will match our price by August 1.
(2) The seller will assume all shipping charges.
(3) The shipper will label all flammable merchandise.

Correct: The contract stipulates that
(1) Barko match our price by August 1,
(2) shipping charges be assumed by the seller, and
(3) all flammable merchandise be labeled.

NOTE: The last format, set up as a continuing sentence, is used less often than either of the first two.

THERAPY 9

Punctuate the following sentences.

1. Before talking to his sales team each morning the boss takes two aspirin and a vodka

2. The company's primary product Jemitone is currently marketed under various trade names

3. Our products are marketed for use in Europe a limited market Latin America one of our leading markets Asia Africa and Australia

4. Granted we do want to emphasize that the fight has just begun

5 A five-year search involving six companies across the United States has proven unsuccessful according to the results

6. Our company has a sound balance sheet with no need of near-term financing but the current ratio at

the end of the third quarter of this fiscal year was not what we expected

7. Other leukocytes are natural killer lymphocytes that kill virus-infected cells scavenger cells amplify immune effects

8. Although we have seen little movement so far the predicted stock market gains are possible

9. Because I do not have a crystal ball I cannot predict whether future products will have the same consequences on our sales therefore we are giving you a flat salary despite your efforts in selling

10. The seminar presents a practical indulgent philosophy toward those who work in our company

11. He wanted to know whether to produce the product or to pull the ads from TV

12. This is the last report I intend to write it includes

everything I know on the subjects of finance and manufacturing

13. These packages were shipped Tuesday July 6 to Atlanta Georgia for use in their computer literacy courses accounting courses and typing courses

14. Our building is so cold that they issue wool underwear with the uniforms

15. His tardiness record needs improvement in fact we've taken out the time clock and installed a calendar

16. In their annual reports prepared by my organization we translate big losses to unrealized gains

17. Eulonda should know if at all possible about our lack of progress in gaining support for our incentive-award idea a trip to the Orient

18. To ensure stability at each branch site in Alaska please make sure the job matches the applicant

19. Jody cannot understand the promotion policies around here and to be sure his efforts do not go unnoticed asks for a performance review after each sale

20. If the research results are unfavorable you had better have enough paperwork to show for the effort

21. We're on a time-management program the boss manages to see that we have no time

22. He has a great deal of authority with his job but at home he has control only of whether he drinks tea or coffee where he dumps his garbage and when he breathes

23. In the first report in the subsection entitled "Pricing" we have included all the guidelines you need

24. I cannot identify the source of the expense-reimbursement memo which I think is the most confusing memo ever to arrive on my desk

25. He's the kind of employee who can find a cloud overhanging every silver lining

26. I mailed the book Tuesday morning although it may not have had proper postage

27. He asked me if I knew there would be a price increase June 1

28. He asked me Do you know if there will be a price increase June 1

29. Punctuation dictates meaning doesn't it

10

SPELLING, WORD CHOICE, AND CAPITALIZATION

If you have a word processor, use your spellchecker—but don't depend on it. In addition to a writer's lack of awareness or laziness or haste, misspellings slip by because computer spellcheckers don't catch errors such as the wrong word *their* for *there*. Therefore, this chapter will primarily focus on the kinds of errors spellcheckers may not correct.

For example, when you write a sentence such as "The new policy will *effect* the employees who have begun work since June 1," you have misused, not simply misspelled, a word. *Effect* as a verb means *to cause;* as a noun, it means *a result*. *Affect* as a verb means *to influence* or *to involve*; as a noun, it mean *an emotion*.

Correct:	This policy will effect (cause) a change.
Correct:	The effect (result) of this policy will be a massive layoff.
Correct:	This policy will affect (influence or in-

volve) those employees who have begun
work since June 1.

To catch these kinds of errors, you need to know the parts of speech discussed in Chapter 1.

Although we have guidelines that attempt to describe the way we spell English words, this chapter will present only a few rules. Spelling rules (such as those involving *ie* or *ei*) have so many exceptions as to make the rules of little value. Therefore, we'll focus on the few indisputable guidelines.

PLURALS

Most nouns are made plural by adding -*s*.

car, car*s*   examination, examinations

Nouns ending in -*sh, -ch, -s,* or -*x* are made plural by adding -*es*.

box, box*es*   loss, loss*es*
church, church*es*   brush, brush*es*

Nouns ending in a silent -*s* do not change their form to become plural.

one corps   one chassis
ten corps   ten chassis

Nouns ending in -*y* preceded by a consonant are made plural by changing the *y* to *i* and adding -*es*.

lady, lad*ies*   county, count*ies*   city, cit*ies*

But nouns ending in -*y* preceded by a vowel are made plural by adding -*s* in the ordinary manner.

    attorney, attorneys   valley, valleys

Many nouns ending in -*f* or -*fe* are made plural by changing the *f* or *fe* to *ves*.

 shelf, shel*ves*   knife, kni*ves*   half, hal*ves*

Some nouns ending in -*o* preceded by a consonant are made plural by adding -*es*.

        potato, potato*es*   hero, hero*es*

But nouns ending in -*o* preceded by a vowel are made plural by adding -*s* in the ordinary manner.

    portfolio, portfolio*s*   studio, studio*s*

Many two-word and three-word compound nouns are made plural by adding -*s* to the base word of the compound.

        commander*s*-in-chief   bill*s* of lading
        accounts receivable

Compound words written as solid words are made plural by adding an -*s* in the ordinary manner.

    courthouse*s*   bookshelve*s*   cutoff*s*

Certain nouns are made plural by a vowel change or the addition of -*en*.

foot, *feet*   woman, wom*en*   child, child*ren*

A few nouns are the same in both singular and plural form.

one deer, two deer   one Chinese, two Chinese
one gross, two gross   one headquarters, two headquarters
one series, two series

Some nouns have no singular form.

measles   politics   news

HOMONYMS AND OTHER MISUSED WORDS

Homonyms are words that sound alike but have different spellings and different meanings (such as *to, too,* and *two*).

He goes *to* work each morning when he can't go back *to* sleep.

He has *too* much retirement built up *to* sleep late.

He has *two* more years of work before he can collect retirement and sleep all day.

Generally, the problem with homonyms is not that writers don't know the difference in meaning but rather that they are careless.

Besides homonyms, we have included other words in the following list that do not sound alike at all. They are included here simply because they are often misused.

accept	(verb—to receive)
except	(preposition—not including)

adapt	(to adjust)
adept	(proficient)
adopt	(to choose)
addition	(something added)
edition	(particular version of a publication)
advice	(noun—counsel)
advise	(verb—to give counsel)
affect	(verb—to influence or to involve)
effect	(verb—to cause; or: noun—a result)
allowed	(permitted)
aloud	(audible)
among	(more than two compared or involved: *among the six of them*)
between	(only two compared or involved; or when more than two things are compared, but each item is compared to one other individually: *between the two of us; between pages of the book*)
amount	(applies to mass or bulk quantities: *an amount of money*)
number	(refers to separate units: *a number of orders*)
apt	(suited, pertinent; inclined to; prompt to learn: *He is apt to accept the promotion.*)
liable	(responsible for consequences: *She is liable for the damages.*)
likely	(probable or probably: *The company will likely fold.*)
as	(introduces a clause: *He left as she entered.*)
like	(introduces a phrase or word: *Like Hortense, Mary too had a problem.*)
assure	(to pledge or give confidence to people—use in the same way as *reassure: He assured us that he would attend.*)

ensure	(to guarantee or make certain—use in cases other than when referring to people: *This new packaging will ensure that the product arrives safely.*)
insure	(to make certain or protect against loss—use when referring to monetary payments: *This bond will insure payment up to $2,000.*)
bare	(without covering)
bear	(noun—an animal; verb—to carry or to hold)
can	(ability to)
may	(permission or possibility)
capital	(adjective—primary, most serious; noun—city, letter, column, accumulated possessions)
capitol	(building)
choose	(present tense of *to choose*—*I always choose the line with the longest wait.*)
chose	(past tense of *to choose*—*I chose that option yesterday.*)
cite	(verb—to give a source)
sight	(noun—eyesight)
site	(noun—a location)
coarse	(texture)
course	(manner, class)
complement	(verb—to make complete; noun—something that completes)
compliment	(verb—to congratulate; noun—praise)
comprise	(to include; avoid following with *of*)
consist of	(to be composed of)
confidant(e)	(a comrade, adviser, friend)
confident	(sure)
continual	(regular, but interrupted)
continuous	(constant and uninterrupted)

credible	(can be reasonably believed: *a credible eyewitness*)
creditable	(deserves praise: *a creditable performance*)
credulous	(believes without reasons, gullible: *a credulous supervisor*)
device	(noun—a plan, procedure, technique, object)
devise	(verb—to plan or to design)
differ from	(unlike—refers to items, ideas, or situations, not people)
differ with	(to disagree—refers to people)
disburse	(to pay out—such as money)
disperse	(to scatter—such as seeds)
disinterested	(impartial)
uninterested	(without interest in)
eligible	(qualified, entitled)
illegible	(undecipherable)
eminent	(outstanding)
imminent	(impending; about to happen)
farther	(physical distance—*two miles farther*)
further	(degree that can't be precisely measured—*two ideas further apart*)
fewer	(use when items can be counted—*fewer letters*)
less	(use with quantities that cannot be counted—*less nitrogen*)
formally	(in a formal manner)
formerly	(previously)
hear	(refers to sound)
here	(refers to location)
heard	(past tense of *to hear*)
herd	(a group)

hours	(time)
ours	(possessive pronoun showing ownership)
in	(within—*The report is in the files.*)
into	(shows motion—*He stepped into the path of the truck.*)
infers	(listener or reader infers—*I infer from her letter that she plans to leave immediately.*)
implies	(speaker or writer implies—*When he talks to each customer, he implies that he is customizing his service.*)
instance	(an example)
instants	(periods of time)
inter-	(prefix meaning between: *intercity*—between cities)
intra-	(prefix meaning within: *intracity*—within one city)
its	(possessive pronoun showing ownership)
it's	(contraction of *it is*)
knew	(past tense of *to know*)
new	(opposite of *old*)
lead	(verb—to be out in front of; noun—position in front; slang for a clue or a tip; marking substance in a pencil; metal)
led	(past tense of *to lead*)
let	(to permit)
leave	(to go away)
lie	(verb—to tell a falsehood *[lie, lied, lied]*; verb—to recline *[lie, lay, lain]*; noun—a falsehood)
lay	(verb—past tense of *to lie* meaning to recline; verb—present tense of *to lay* meaning *to place [lay, laid, laid]:*

I lie about my reasons every day.

I lied yesterday about my reasons.

I lie on the carpet and cry when he walks in.

I lay on the carpet and cried yesterday when he walked in.

I have lain here crying all week.

I lay this contract on your desk every day as a strong hint.

The unsigned contract lay on his desk for a week.

lose	(verb—to fail to win, gain, or obtain)
loose	(adjective—unattached)
loss	(noun—that which is ruined, destroyed, or diminished)
may	(shows possibility)
might	(shows stronger uncertainty than *may*)
might of	(don't use)
might have	(correct)
one	(the number)
won	(past tense of *to win*)
passed	(past tense of *to pass*—We passed the accident site.)
past	(period of time before the present; never a verb)
peace	(without turmoil)
piece	(a portion of)
pear	(fruit)
pare	(to reduce)
pair	(couple)
perspective	(viewpoint)
prospective	(likely to become; expected)
persecute	(to oppress)
prosecute	(to bring legal charges against)

plain	(adjective—simple, ordinary; noun—level, treeless countryside)
plane	(noun—an airplane, a tool; verb—to level)
practical	(useful or workable as opposed to theoretical)
practicable	(possible or feasible)
precede	(to go before—*Chapter 2 precedes Chapter 3.*)
proceed	(to move ahead—*Let's proceed with the plan.*)
principal	(adjective—chief, primary; noun—one who has control)
principle	(a rule or guideline)
quiet	(adjective—without noise or disturbance)
quite	(adverb—completely, positively, rather)
quit	(verb—to stop)
red	(color)
read	(verb—both present and past tense of *to read. I read the reports every day. I read the reports yesterday.*)
speak to	(to tell; to greet)
speak with	(to discuss)
stationary	(immobile)
stationery	(writing material)
teach	(to instruct)
learn	(to gain knowledge or understanding)
tenant	(one who rents property)
tenet	(a rule or principle)
than	(conjunction that compares; used to link words, phrases, or clauses—*He knows more than I do.*)
then	(adverb—tells when)

their	(possessive pronoun showing owner-ship)
there	(adverb telling where; an expletive—*There was a problem.*)
they're	(contraction of *they are*)

threw	(verb—past tense of *to throw*)
through	(preposition—by, because of, from beginning to end)
thorough	(adjective—complete, comprehensive)

| unless | (preposition or conjunction connecting two clauses—*He can't resign unless I say so. Without* would be incorrect in this sentence.) |
| without | (preposition that must be followed by an object or an objective phrase—*He left without permission.*) |

| use to | (don't use) |
| used to | (correct) |

| wait | (verb—to pause or to delay) |
| weight | (noun—mass, load; verb—to load or to make heavy) |

| weak | (without strength) |
| week | (seven days) |

| who's | (contraction of *who is*) |
| whose | (possessive pronoun showing owner-ship) |

| your | (possessive pronoun showing owner-ship) |
| you're | (contraction of *you are*) |

CAPITALIZATION

If you intend to emphasize a word, do not simply capitalize the first letter. Instead, bold print it, underline it, italicize it, or write the entire word in uppercase. Capitalize only for the following reasons:

Proper Nouns

Capitalize words that refer specifically by name.

People:	Hortense H. Hupplenicker
Places:	Minneapolis the Midwest Florida Chesapeake Bay Columbia Avenue the Middle East the Oval Office Mount Vernon
Races and Languages:	Caucasian Spanish
Days of the Week, Months, Special Days (not seasons):	Tuesday July Easter Halloween
Historical Periods and Events:	the Roaring Twenties the Great Depression the Dark Ages
Trade Names:	Plexiglas, Corning Ware
Deity:	Son of God, Christ
Companies:	IBM has developed a state-of-the-art software package for your application. Our company is trying to mimic that IBM software package. (The word *company* in the second sentence is not capitalized even though the writer is referring specifically to a particular company. The writer used only a generic reference to the company, not the specific company name.)

NOTE: You may capitalize words such as *company, bank, organization*, or *buyer* in documents such as formal policy statements or contracts when these words have first been identified in full and when they are used as "nicknames" throughout the remainder of the document.

Mr. and Mrs. Jenzenne Jabwok, hereafter referred to as Buyers, deny all claims. Additionally, Buyers will provide . . .

First National Bank (later referred to as Bank) will not assume liability in the following cases:
1. When Bank gives written notice of foreclosure
2. When Bank has no power of attorney

Positions or Job Titles

Capitalize a position title only when it *precedes* a name as a person's specific title. Do not capitalize a title when it follows or replaces a name.

John Dasharound, vice president of marketing, has signed the agreement.

Vice President of Marketing John Dasharound has signed the agreement.

Do not capitalize a generic reference to a position or organization.

All the senators think . . .
Our club voted . . .
Company officials today predicted that . . .

NOTE: Do capitalize titles of state, federal, or international officials of high distinction such as the President of the United States or cabinet members (but not local or company officials).

Other Uses of Capitalization

First Letters of Sentences

The telephone is the biggest time-saver and time-waster ever invented.

First Word of Direct Quotes

The contract specifically states, "We will not engage in litigation involving Anwart Inc."

NOTE: Do not capitalize the first word of a direct quote if it continues, rather than begins, a sentence.

Your boss admitted that she was "sick and tired" of your attitude.

First Word of Independent Questions Within Sentences

The issue is, Will this mean a larger profit? (Also correct: *The issue is, will . . .?*)

First Word of Items in a Formal List

Here are items you will need to bring to our meeting:

- Calculator
- Previous contracts
- Departmental policy statements
- Aspirin

First Word and All Principal Words in Headings or Titles

The Economic Disaster of the
Research Department

The Foggy Fortress of Finance is a 500-page book that advises little more than to stay out of the stock market. This book also suggests that investors stay away from tax-exempt bonds. (Even though the second sentence refers specifically to the earlier named book, the book is not called by its title in the second sentence. Therefore, *book* should not be capitalized.)

NOTE: Do not capitalize *a*, *an*, or *the* or prepositions of fewer than four letters such as *in*, *by*, or *for* unless they are the first or last word of a heading or a title.

First Word of Each Line of Poetry

> Budgets are red,
> People are blue.
> I'm tired of this,
> How about you?

First and Principal Words in Addresses

> John True, Vice Chairman
> Department of Finance
> 1122 Shogun
> Knowntown, TX

First Words in Salutations and Closings

> Dear John,
> My dear Mr. Snodgrass:
> Sincerely yours,

I, Oh

> Yes, I am willing to accept a raise if that will make you feel better about my performance.

> You're giving me a raise; Oh, how nice!

APOSTROPHES

Many other grammar books consider apostrophes and hyphens as "word punctuation" and include those guidelines in chapters on general punctuation. But I've found that most writers think of apostrophes and hyphenation as a part of spelling. Therefore, I've included them here.

Apostrophes primarily show ownership; however, they do have other uses as explained in the following sections:

To Show Possession

Singular Nouns

doctor's nurse	receptionist's desk	Mike's report
Chris's contract	manager's resignation	client's hint

Plurals Ending with a Letter Other Than -s

children's royalties   businessmen's suits
women's rights

Plurals Ending with -s

employees' benefits   stockholders' position
lawyers' caseloads   managers' agreement

NOTE: Some authorities add the extra -*s* even on singular words already ending in -*s*. Generally, prefer omitting the additional -*s* after the apostrophe when the -*s's* would run together and cause a hissing, awkward sound.

In general, just remember to make the word singular or plural first and then show ownership by adding only the apostrophe or an apostrophe and an additional -*s*.

instructor's staff (One instructor)
instructors' staff (More than one instructor. The extra syllable on this possessive is not pronounced, so the final -s is dropped.)

NOTE: A noun does not necessarily have to follow the possessive word.

The decision was Jill's.

NOTE: Be sure to distinguish between words used to describe as opposed to those used to show possession. Either of the following uses is correct, depending on your meaning. Choose one style and be consistent in a single document.

the Department of Defense plan (descriptive)
the Department of Defense's plan (ownership)
the users manual (descriptive)
the user's manual (ownership)
the client and the vendor contracts (descriptive)
the client's and the vendor's contracts (ownership)
attorneys meeting—2 p.m. (This refers to a meeting *for* attorneys, not owned by attorneys. However, if attorneys called the meeting, are in charge of the meeting, and in a sense "own" the meeting, you may correctly write *attorneys' meeting*.)

Some organizations and publications use apostrophes in their titles; others do not.

Reader's Digest
Writer's Digest
Boys' Life
Young Women's
    Christian Organization

Publishers Weekly
Ladies Home Journal
American Bankers
    Association
National Speakers
    Association

NOTE: Don't make careless errors such as placing an apostrophe in the middle of the word or using an apostrophe simply to show the plural form of a noun.

Incorrect:	Jone's contract (The full name is *Jones*.)
Incorrect:	We walked past three vacant lot's. (*Lots* is the simple plural—no ownership is involved.)

Joint Ownership

Joe Blucksky's and Susan Susquachful's work is complete. (Two different projects)

Joe Blucksky and Susan Susquachful's work is complete. (One project. They worked on the project together.)

Connection, Attribute, or Duration

a month's salary four years' experience
conscience' sake women's issues

Possessive Case of Pronouns

Do not use an apostrophe to show the possessive case of pronouns. These pronouns are already possessive:

hers his yours theirs ours its

Don't confuse the word *it's* (contraction of *it is*) with *its* (pronoun showing ownership).

Possessives Before Gerunds

We could not explain *John's* designating the area around the water cooler for "working" employees.

Remember that a gerund is a verb ending in -*ing* that functions as a noun. Substitute another noun for the gerund here to understand why *John* must be possessive: *We could not explain John's decision.*

To Indicate Missing Letters or Numbers

In addition to showing ownership, apostrophes represent missing letters in contractions and sometimes in abbreviations.

can't   I'll   ma'am   the class of '88

To Show the Plural of Abbreviations, Figures, and Letters Referred to As Words

Your layout of this section is inconsistent with the *b's* used as subheads elsewhere.

The *8's* in this typescript resemble *3's*.

The *and's* in this contract are vague linking words.

They began the policy in the *1970's* (or *1970s*).

We've had *VIP's* (or *VIPs*) all around the office this morning.

NOTE: In many cases such as these, the apostrophe is optional. Let clarity be your guide. For instance,

Send us the following pumps:

- 3—model 126ds
- 2—model WPRs

Where do the serial number and letter identifications end? Is the final -*s* on the letters and numbers in the preceding example part of the model identification? Or does the final

-*s* only make the identifications plural? In such cases, an apostrophe clearly means plural:

- 3—model 126d's (more than one model 126d).
- 2—model WPR's (more than one model WPR).

HYPHENATION

Prefixes and Suffixes

Rules about hyphenation change frequently. When two words are first used together or when prefixes and suffixes are first placed with a root word, the resulting compound is written with a hyphen. However, as the compound becomes more commonplace in the language, we gradually drop the hyphen and write the two root words or the root and its prefix or suffix together. Very few prefixes and suffixes in our language still require a hyphen (*ex-*, *quasi-*, *self-*, *all-*, *-elect*). Other prefixes and suffixes, such as the following ones, are now written as one.

powerlessness	fortyish	pseudointellectual
nonessential	updated	pretest
intramural	interstate	reexamine
unnecessary	semiannual	coordination
contrariwise	subcommittee	substandard
foursquare	clockwise	halfhearted
globelike	threefold	twosome

NOTE: Always use a hyphen between a prefix and a root word to prevent misreading (reform/re-form; recreation/re-creation).

She tried to *re-cover* the typewriter. (She tried to cover the typewriter again.)

She tried to *recover* the typewriter. (She tried to get the typewriter from the person who took it.)

NOTE: Hyphenate a prefix if the root word is capitalized.

The orgy begins in mid-August.

According to my boss, loneliness is un-American.

Despite the broad guideline that hyphens drop out of compounds as the compounds become more widely used, we do have the following few specific rules about hyphenation.

Related Adjectives and Adverbs

Hyphenate two or more words combined as an adjective to be used as a unit preceding a noun. If the adjectives follow a noun, do not hyphenate them unless they are in an altered or inverted form.

He gave us an off-the-record report.
His report is off the record.

Ours is a pay-as-you-go plan.
Our plan allows you to pay as you go.

But:

This has been a user-tested product.
This product has been user-tested. (Retain the hyphen in altered form. Normal order: *tested by users*)

He bought a tax-exempt bond.
The bond he bought was tax-exempt. (Retain the hyphen in altered form. Normal order: *exempt from taxes*)

NOTE: Some related adjectives used as a single unit are not hyphenated because the two modifiers represent a single concept and are clear without hyphens.

Hire a good *real estate agent*.
He wants to attend a *supervisory skills course*.

He practices his fiction in preparing *income tax returns*.

The *sodium chloride solution* has been labeled.

Let clarity be your guide:

Bob is an old car buff. (Is he an elderly man who knows a lot about cars, or is he a man who knows about old cars? *Bob is an old-car buff*.)

He ordered six inch razors. (Did he order six razors an inch long, or did he order razors six inches long? *He ordered six-inch razors*.)

In general, do not hyphenate adverb-adjective combinations. Adverbs modify adjectives, not nouns.

Incorrect: This seminar is a highly-rated educational program.

The only exception to the adverb-adjective hyphenation rule is with the adverbs *well* and *less*. Like two related adjectives, these combinations require a hyphen when they precede a noun; they do not require a hyphen when they follow a noun.

Amherst is a well-known company.
Amherst is well known.

This is a less-acceptable solution.
This solution is less acceptable.

Suspended Hyphens

When two or more prefixes or adjectives are linked to the same term, use a suspended hyphen after each prefix or word of the series.

Complete both the pre- and post-questionnaires.

We have reached neither our short- nor our long-term objectives.

Compound Numbers

Hyphenate compound numbers from twenty-one to ninety-nine:

twenty-two   forty-eight   sixty-four

Compound Words

Hyphenate compound words that do not have a noun as their base word:

go-between   higher-ups   know-it-all

For more specific hyphenation guidelines, check a recent dictionary.

ONE WORD OR TWO?

Writers sometimes become confused with words that can be written either as one compound word or as two words.

anymore	vs.	any more
sometime	vs.	some time
maybe	vs.	may be
anyway	vs.	any way

The key to the one-word or two-word dilemma is identifying what part of speech you need. (I told you that knowing parts of speech would come in handy.) If the occasion calls for only one part of speech, write the word as a compound. Most such compounds are adverbs.

He doesn't care *anymore*. (Adverb—*how* he cares—not much)

Drop by and see me *sometime*. (Adverb—*when* to drop by)

Maybe we can go today. (Adverb—*possibly*)

To decide if you need two words (two parts of speech), reword your sentence and see if part of the compound changes. If so, you know you need to write the idea as two words.

He doesn't have *any more* pencils. (Reword: *He may have two more or three more. Any* is an adverb; *more* is a pronoun meaning pencils in the reworded sentence.)

Do you have *some time* this afternoon? (Reword: *Yes, I have a little time. Some* is an adjective; *time* is a noun.)

This *may be* the answer to our problem. (Reword: *And then, it may not be the answer. May be* is the verb phrase; *not* is an adverb.)

Do not use hyphens in the following verb forms. Such words may or may not require hyphens when used as adjectives or nouns.

Please *follow up* his progress.
(His *follow-up* [adjective] report is due Tuesday.)

Go ahead with your plans.
(She gave me the *go-ahead* [noun] on my plans.)

These tables *break down* all expenses by branch office.
(I need a *breakdown* [noun] on all expenses by branch office.)

ITALICS

Use italics (shown by underlining in typewriting) to show emphasis.

Please try to imitate what I *say*, not what I *do*.

Use italics for foreign abbreviations, words, and phrases.

He insisted that his briefcase purchase was *à bon marché*.

Italics are no longer necessary for words that have become common in English.

I think you can accurately consider your comment to the president a faux pas.

He insists that this is a bona fide offer.

Use italics to indicate separately published works.

the *Houston Chronicle*
Megatrends
Symposium on Space: Volume 2
My White House Years
Bulletin D212

Use italics to indicate a word, letter, or number as such.

He insists that the *and* be removed from the second sentence in the contract.

Use italics for names of ships, aircraft, and spacecraft.

the shuttle *Challenger*
U.S.S. *Enterprise*
the *Washingtonian*

Use italics for *Resolved* and *Provided* in resolutions and
legislative acts.

Resolved, That the company president be allowed to
keep her job . . .

We agree to pay $10 million, *Provided,* That . . .

THERAPY 10

See if you can spot the errors (capitalization, hyphenation, apostrophes, misused words) in the following sentences.

1. Our ℂompany demands confidentiality in these direct mail campaigns.

2. He has never received a promotion since working
   their; he attributes his lack of success to the fact
   that he was born on Friday, February 13.

3. He does not seem too understand the problem well
   enough to present any solution.

4. The manager has outlined a step by step approach
   for failure.

5. I think you can say our company is over regulated. We have sixty six Policies for operating the elevators' safely.

6. The door's in our office building, to, do not yet have signs; its difficult, therefore, too distinguish restrooms from storage closets.

7. He says that may be the plan will work and may be it won't.

8. The three supervisors status reports reflect they're attitudes about the problem approach.

9. Mr. Johnson ensures us that we will get their business.

10. Donald Blumberhead is a Manager who's experience qualifies him only to empty the garbage.

11

OTHER THINGS THAT MAY RAISE EYEBROWS

SPLIT INFINITIVES

Years ago a split infinitive was a sin punishable by the task of rewriting a composition. Today split infinitives are considered questionable, but excusable with good reason. (Remember, an infinitive is the word *to* plus a verb.) For example, you can write—

To understand this problem *really*, you must be a member of the team. (Awkward)

Really to understand this problem, you must be a member of the team. (Awkward)

To *really* understand this problem, you must be a member of the team. (Adds emphasis)

This technique will help you to *effectively* end each sales call. (Unnecessary split)

This technique will help you to end each sales call *effectively*. (Better)

This escapade should help you to *indefinitely* prolong the project. (Unnecessary split)

This technique will help you to prolong the project *indefinitely*. (Better)

To sum up: Split your infinitives only for a very good reason.

PREPOSITIONS THAT END SENTENCES

You may have had an English teacher who said, "Never end a sentence with a preposition." This is generally good advice. But definitely you must break the rule on occasion when alternate constructions sound more awkward than the prepositional ending.

He is the man I spoke with. (Okay, but sounds limp—use when speaking and writing informally)

He is the man with whom I spoke. (Okay, but sounds stuffy—use when speaking and writing on formal occasions)

When I prepare the invitation list for the retirement luncheon, on how many guests should I count? (Awkward—will the writer count on bodies of the guests?)

When I prepare the invitation list for the retirement luncheon, how many guests should I count on? (Better)

This is something into which you should check. (Ridiculous and ambiguous—such as a hotel maybe?)

This is something you should check into. (Limp)

You should check into this. (Better)

These are the designs on which I worked. (Stuffy and ambiguous—Did you stand on the designs?)

These are the designs I worked on. (Limp)

I worked on these designs. (Better)

As you can see, sentences that end in prepositions may sound flimsy at the end. On the other hand, some sentences sound awkward or are ambiguous when you reconstruct them to avoid the prepositional ending. When either is the case, you may end your sentences with a preposition without fear of condemnation.

DOUBLE NEGATIVES

There are no exceptions about this taboo. Do not use more than one negative within the same clause. (Negatives: *no, not, nor, neither, none, never, no one, hardly, scarcely*)

Incorrect:	She *has never* had *no* worries.
Correct:	She has *never* had *any* worries.
	She has had *no* worries.

| **Incorrect:** | She *scarcely* had *no* money left. |
| **Correct:** | She *scarcely* had *any* money left. |

| **Incorrect:** | He *hardly never* calls for a favor. |
| **Correct:** | He *hardly ever* calls for a favor. |

Incorrect:	He does*n't* have *no* authority in this situation.
Correct:	He does*n't* have *any* authority in this situation.
	He has *no* authority in this situation.

| **Incorrect:** | We *never* have *no* advance warning about power failures. |
| **Correct:** | We have *no* advance warning about power failures. |

We *never* have *any* advance warning about power failures.

Incorrect: We did *not* find nails *nor* screws at the scene.

Correct: We did *not* find nails *or* screws at the scene.

We found *neither* nails *nor* screws at the scene.

(*Neither/nor* go together as linking words; this is not a double-negative construction.)

Incorrect: The operator could*n't* give us *no* news.

Correct: The operator could*n't* give us *any* news.

The operator *could* give us *no* news.

You ai*n't* going to need *no* more help with this *neither*, are you *not*?

THAT VERSUS *WHICH*

It may comfort you to know that in the distant past careful writers always made a distinction between *that* and *which*. However, because of "exceptions" to their primary, common use and because of flagrant misuse, the distinction between the two words has become hazy. Generally, you should use *that* to introduce essential clauses and *which* to introduce nonessential clauses.

He called about the invoice that I enclosed in the box. (The *that* clause points out a specific invoice.)

He called about the invoice, which I enclosed in the box. (The *which* clause only adds information—the fact that the writer enclosed the invoice. The *which* clause does *not* distinguish one invoice from another invoice; therefore, the *which* clause is nonessential.)

Jeff bought the product that I first demonstrated. (Jeff bought the product that I first demonstrated as opposed to the second product that I demonstrated. The *that* clause is essential to identify the specific product.)

Jeff bought the product, which I first demonstrated. (The main idea is that Jeff bought the product. The nonessential *which* clause only adds information about who first demonstrated the product.)

I proofread all the brochures that contain errors. (The *that* clause points out specific brochures; it is essential to the full meaning.)

I proofread all the brochures, which contain errors. (The nonessential *which* clause merely adds a thought; we already know which brochures.)

You'll note from the above examples that *that* clauses have no commas. *Which* clauses usually require commas because they add nonessential information.

Now, here is the problem: The above general rules about *that* and *which* hold true with these exceptions: If you have a sentence that has two *that* clauses, you may change one of the *thats* to *which*.

She went out to buy a style book *that* includes colloquialisms *which* she frequently uses. (The *which* can be *that;* the writer simply changes to *which* to avoid repetition of *that*.)

A second exception is a situation in which *that* follows a preposition; you must change the *that* to *of which*.

He has created this pandemonium *of which* I cannot speak.

Be aware that the choice between *that* and *which* affects

punctuation. You will be safe to remember that a comma separating the clause from the rest of the sentence means that the clause adds nonessential information. Without the comma to cut the idea away, the clause restricts the meaning of the words that precede the *that* or *which*.

Correct:	Higher prices cut into purchasing power, which I don't have after the 20th of each month. (Nonessential clause—The writer has no purchasing power after the 20th.)
Correct:	Higher prices cut into purchasing power that I don't have after the 20th of each month. (Essential clause—The writer's specific purchasing power is affected by higher prices.)

All that is to say this: You need to know the uses of a comma to set off *that* and *which* clauses because people often use these pronouns interchangeably. (If you still have problems with essential and nonessential clauses, review the comma section of Chapter 9.)

RELATIVE PRONOUN PROBLEMS

Who and *whom* refer only to persons. *Which* refers to animals and things. *That* can refer to persons, animals, or things.

The question also frequently arises: When may I omit the relative pronoun *that?*

He said he wanted your signature today.
He said *that* he wanted your signature today.

In the above example, you have a choice; the sentence is clear with or without the pronoun *that* to introduce the noun clause. Choose whichever sounds better to your ear.

There is one situation, however, that does call for the pronoun *that*—when a "time" word comes between the verb and the clause.

Unclear:	The boss reported Tuesday sales fluttered a little. (Did the boss report on Tuesday, or did sales flutter on Tuesday?)
Clear:	The boss reported *that* Tuesday sales fluttered a little.
Clear:	The boss reported Tuesday *that* sales fluttered a little.

Another problem with the relative pronoun *which* is that *which* should stand for a specific noun in most sentences. Some writers dangle *which* clauses on the end of sentences to refer to the entire previously stated idea. In other words, the *which* in the following unclear sentences means "that fact."

Unclear:	I do not understand all the technicalities, which is why I transferred to a new job. (Why the transfer? The technicalities or lack of understanding about the technicalities?)
Better:	I do not understand all the technicalities; this lack of expertise is why I transferred to a new job.
Unclear:	The contract needs to be signed this week, which makes it urgent that I locate Brenda Brown immediately. (The contract or the short deadline makes it urgent?)
Better:	The contract needs to be signed this week. This short deadline makes it urgent that I locate Brenda Brown immediately.
Unclear:	We shipped the order last October, which

is why we are wondering why we've not received your payment.

Better: Because we shipped your order last October, we are wondering why we've not received your payment.

We shipped the order last October; therefore, we are wondering why we've not received your payment.

Unclear: My boss can't remember names, which is why she offends most of her clients.

Better: My boss can't remember names and thus offends most of her clients.

Most of my boss's clients feel offended because she can't remember their names.

UNEQUAL, AMBIGUOUS, OR INCOMPLETE COMPARISONS

Don't mix metaphors. Don't allude to things or conditions you are comparing without completing the thought in writing. Some adjectives and adverbs (such as *unique, round, never,* or *perfect*) cannot logically be compared at all because of their meanings.

With this problem, he can't get to first base or persuade management to roll with the punches a while longer. (Mixed metaphor—baseball and boxing)

Gertrude seems to have more confidence. (More confidence than she has what? Or: More confidence than who?)

He has a more unique approach than mine. (*Unique* means one of a kind. Either his approach is unique or it isn't.)

This is a longer report. (Longer than what?)

This year's sales are lower than last year. (Are the sales

lower than the year? Correct: *This year's sales are lower than last year's*.)

The boss hates visitors as much as her husband. (Does the boss hate visitors *and* her husband? Does the boss's husband also hate visitors? Correct: *The boss hates visitors as much as her husband does*.)

UNCLEAR REFERENCES

Be wary of sentences or clauses that begin with *this, that, they, it,* or *which* when these pronouns can refer to more than one previously mentioned noun. If there is more than one word these pronouns can logically refer to, you should repeat the noun.

Unclear:	The results were a big disappointment to the committee members, and *they* have delayed further action. (Who or what does *they* refer to—the results or the committee members?)
Clear:	The results were a big disappointment to the committee members; therefore, *the members* have delayed further action.
Unclear:	I took the distance into consideration when I performed the analysis, *which* shows that the decision is not a good one. (What shows that the decision is not a good one—the analysis or the distance?)
Clear:	I took the distance into consideration when I performed the analysis, and *the analysis* shows that the decision is not a good one.
Unclear:	The increase in the attrition rate at least has solved our problems of office space, compensation, and sales-call expense. *This* is something that should be given further consideration. (What should be

given further consideration? The increase in the attrition rate? The space problem? The compensation problem? The sales-call expense? Or the relationship between the attrition rate and these three things?)

Clear: The increase in the attrition rate at least has solved our problems of office space, compensation, and sales-call expense. The *relationship between the attrition rate and these three problems* should be given further consideration.

UNNECESSARY PREPOSITIONS

Did your mother ever use this line on you when correcting your grammar?

You: Where is Eddie at?
Her: Between the *a* and the *t*.

If you've heard this little ditty but missed the point, here it is: Omit prepositions that add nothing to the meaning of the sentence.

Where did the contract go (to)?

I could not help (from) crying over my raise.

She sauntered outside (of) the building in the rain.

My desk is opposite (of) yours.

It is too near (to) lunch to leave work sick.

The box fell off (of) the cart during transport.

PARALLELISM

We discussed parallelism in the Major Relapses section of Chapter 3. Parallelism means simply that you should present equal ideas in similar sentence structure—all prepositional phrases, all clauses, all verbals, etc.

Unparallel:	Give me liberty or I'm willing to negotiate.
Parallel:	Give me liberty or give me death.
Unparallel:	Before resigning your job, consider these things: educational opportunities, how large your savings account is, references, the unemployment rates.
Parallel:	Before resigning your job, consider these things: educational opportunities, the size of your savings account, references, unemployment rates.
Unparallel:	Harvey told me to disconnect the phone and that I should lock all outside doors.
Parallel:	Harvey told me to disconnect the phone and to lock all outside doors.
Parallel:	Harvey told me that I should disconnect the phone and lock all outside doors.

DANGLERS

Danglers can be demons. Remember to attach modifying words and phrases logically to the words they describe.

Dangler:	The report has several discrepancies, calculating the temperatures according to my charts. (Did the report calculate the temperatures?)
Correct:	Calculating the temperatures according to my charts, I find several discrepancies in the report.
Dangler:	While writing my resume, they filled the position. (Were they writing your resume?)
Correct:	While writing my resume, I found that the position had been filled.

THERAPY 11

Identify and correct things in the following sentences that may raise eyebrows—questionable or incorrect constructions.

1. You have to be computer literate to ~~really~~ foul things up .

2. We haven't never said that this product was no good.

3. He made an issue of pointing out all the mistakes, which should not have upset the writer.

4. The telegrams he sends always get results. However, they may be expensive.

5. The director has assigned me to correct the problem, which my boss sees as an advantage.

6. He suggested more water coolers and that we give employees shorter work periods between breaks.

7. Please take a moment to thoroughly read this chapter in case your next boss is a former English teacher.

8. Let me know if I can help you and the results.

9. You should have picked up the application blank which allows you to enter the sales contest. [The application blank is a specific one for entering the sales contest as opposed to another application blank for requesting permission to attend the seminar.]

10. I want to ultimately verify all such claims of sanity.

11. We can always hope for an increase in salary and to get a longer vacation.

12. Sparky Skymouth is the employee which I hired the morning of my hangover.

13. The slump in sales has resulted in our getting the

new advertising contract; that is something we need to discuss in our Friday meeting.

14. I did not see neither the letter or the resume.

15. The blueprints do not refer to the DPX number, the invoice number, or what number is on the order.

16. While away at the conference, my desk was moved into the hallway.

17. He suggested revising the rules of the sales campaign or that we could eliminate employee participation.

18. After forcing my opinion down his throat, the discussion was postponed.

19. I could not handle the problem, which he realized.

20. These reports are clearer than last month.

21. Your questions are outside of my area of expertise.

12

VISUALS

The first few "pictures" that follow will give you the key to understanding the sentence diagrams:

| Subject | verb | object |

| Subject | verb \ subject complement |

| Subject | verb | object \ object complement |

Compound subjects and compound verbs

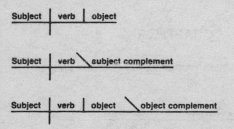

Infinitives   Participles   Gerunds

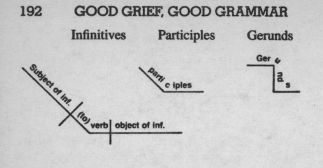

Modifiers hang below the words they modify.

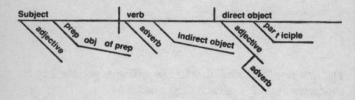

CHAPTER 2

1. My boss has been preparing his overdue resignation.

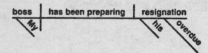

2. He considers team sports an unnecessary time-waster.

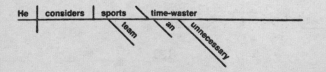

3. These chemicals smell bad and taste poisonous.

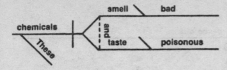

4. Candidly, the systems and design engineer, Muriel Hangover, made the project even more difficult.

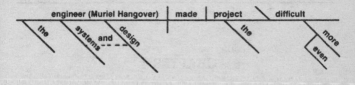

CHAPTER 3

5. He walked into the conference room with down-cast eyes and open hands.

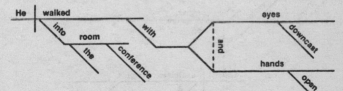

6. In the winner's circle is where I want to be.

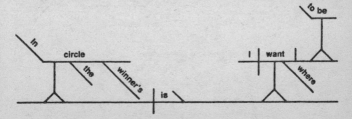

7. Overstatement is always more dangerous than understatement.

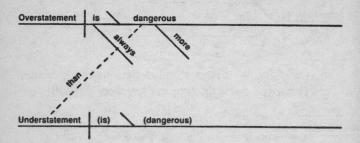

CHAPTER 4

8. These provisions are strictly enforced by the company, which from time to time exercises its right
to do stupid things.

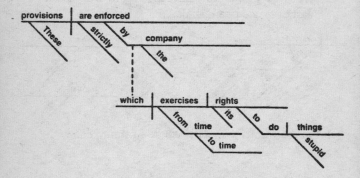

9. Tell me how you sold that merchandise, and I'll tell you how I figured your commission.

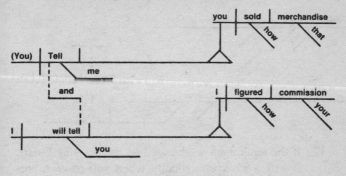

CHAPTER 5

10. He practiced the presentation thoroughly, he prepared the proper visuals, and then he pulverized the main points before his top-management audience.

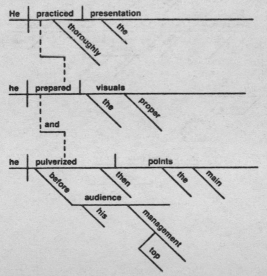

11. She did not get a raise because she had the nerve to think that she deserved it.

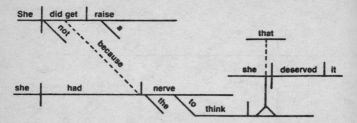

12. If the equipment works well on the drawing board, it will work spasmodically when you make a presentation to management; it will not work at all when you demonstrate it to the customer.

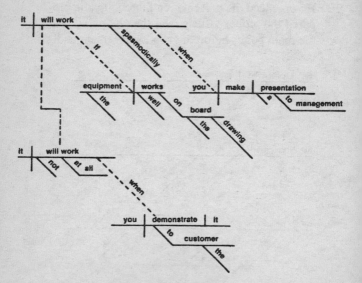

ANSWERS TO QUIZZES

INTRODUCTION

Errors marked in opening paragraphs:

The room looked like a funeral parlor trans-

capitaliza-
tion error

planted to the tallest Skyscraper in Houston.

The executives marched in one by one, eyes

downcast and briefcases swishing to the table-

top with clicking sounds as locks opened.

comma
error

John Clayton, program analyst‸knew this

dangling
verbal

meeting would be the turning point. (Assuming

they would come to a decision today) the out-

misused
word

come would ~~effect~~ affect his career, his marriage,

parallelism
error

and probably determine the day of his murder.

197

capitalization error	The Senior Vice President took his seat at
semicolon error	the end of the conference table, and the other
misused word	assorted company officers followed his ~~led~~ lead
comma error	and shuffled into place. John kept his face
apostrophe error	blank as Mary's airline tickets slid to the floor
pronoun agreement	with a slight flutter. He nonchalantly retrieved
misused prep.	(it) and tucked (it) back ~~in~~ into his coat pocket. He
comma error	began to wonder, why he'd (only bought) her
misplaced modifier	ticket and not his also. Had he subconsciously
	already made his decision weeks ago—before
	the audit, before the programmers had cracked
parallelism error	the code, and perhaps even before the $2 million shipment of size 10 negligees?

THERAPY 1

Using the simple abbreviations here, label each word in the following sentences as to its part of speech.

noun—n	verb—v	adjective–adj
adverb—adv	conjunction—cj	interjection—ij
pronoun—pn	preposition—pp	

```
    pn   v       adj adj  adj   n   pp   n
 1. I exhausted all my good ideas by noon.
```

adj   n   v   v   adv
2. The invoice was calculated incorrectly.

adj   adj   n   v   adj   n   pp
3. This caustic letter denounces the deficiency in
   n   pp   adj   n
brainpower around our office.

   pp   pp adj   adj   n   adv pn v pn
4. Regardless of the stupid ideas here, we thank you
pp adj n
for your letter.

adj   n   cj adj adj   n   v
5. The committee and my three assistants have
   v   pp adj   adj   n   adv   pp
worked on the quarterly report diligently against
adj   n   cj   pp adj   adj   n
false deadlines and despite other daily projects.

   pp   adj   n   pn v   adv
6. With experienced personnel, we can professionally
   v   adj   n   cj pp adj   n
examine all foodstuffs and, by minor repair, im-
v   adj adj   n   cj   n
prove the surface imperfections before customers
   v cj v pn
buy and eat them.

   v   adj   n   cj   adv   v   cj
7. Downgrade the service and improperly install and
   v   adj n   pp   n   cj pn v
identify each piece of equipment as we have pre-
adv   v
viously authorized.

    n   n   v   v   adj n pp adj

8. Jeffrey Smarts has accumulated the data for the

    n   pp   n   n

meeting with Freda Flabbergasted.

    adj   n   v adj adj pn

9. This situation is a dismal one.

    n   n   v pn adj n   pp adj   n

10. John Tactless sent them a memo about his philoso-

          pp   n   cj   adv   v adj

phy of management and, consequently, ensured his

    adj   n

sudden departure.

    cj   pn v v adj   n   pp adj   n

11. Either they will try my suggestion for rainy weather

    cj   pn   v   v adv adj

or someone must be all wet.

    cj pn v pp   n   v   pn

12. If you are in doubt, fire someone.

    pp adj   n   adj   n   pp   adj   n

13. In our company, the difference between sales rep

       cj   n   pp   n   v adv adj adj   n

and director of marketing is about two good sales.

    adj   adj   n   v   adj   n

14. Our company policy mandates safety inspections

    adj   adj   n

every twenty years.

    adj   adj   n   v   pn   pp

15. His activity report indicates everything except ac-

    n

tivity.

16.   pn   v   n   pp adj adj   adj
    She loses enthusiasm with each new product bro-
     n
    chure.

17.   n   v adj adj   n   pp adj   n   pp
    Gertrude was the role model for his book on fail-
     n
    ure.

18.   pp   adj   n   n   v   n   cj
    To most people, paperwork ensures delay and
     v   n
    offers self-protection.

19.   pp   adj   n   pp adj   adj   n   cj
    Despite our installation of a voice-mail system and
          adj   n   adj   n   v adv
    videoconferencing equipment, the grapevine is still
    adj   adj   n   pp adj   n
    our fastest mode of internal communication.

THERAPY 2

In the following sentences, label each underlined word according to its sentence function. You have already had some practice in labeling verbs, adjectives, and adverbs in Chapter 1; in these instances, the part of speech is the same as the sentence function. Therefore, note that the adjective and adverb modifiers in these sentences are not underlined.

subject—s   subject complement—sc
verb (predicate)—v   object complement—oc
appositive—app   noun of direct address—nda
direct object—do   indirect object—io

1. Willetta Weightlossinzsky **types** Margaret Nospell-
   checker's audit **reports**.

   [s over Willetta Weightlossinzsky, v over types, do over reports]

2. ✍ My **boss** **has been preparing** his overdue **resignation**.

   [s over boss, v over has been preparing, do over resignation]

3. My **price** **is** **cheap**.

   [s over price, v over is, sc over cheap]

4. **I** **will give** **you** an **answer** today.

   [s over I, v over will give, io over you, do over answer]

5. ✍ **He** **considers** team **sports** an unnecessary **time-
   waster**.

   [s over He, v over considers, do over sports, oc over waster]

6. Douglas **Donothing**, a management **consultant**, **sent**
   the **group** a shocking **invoice**.

   [s over Donothing, app over consultant, v over sent, io over group, do over invoice]

7. **Margie**, **did** **you** **take** this **call**?

   [nda over Margie, v over did, s over you, v over take, do over call]

8. There **must be** a **problem**.

   [v over must be, s over problem]

9. **Someone** **is** always **exercising** his option **clause**.

   [s over Someone, v over is, v over exercising, do over clause]

10. ✍ These chemicals smell bad and taste poisonous.
    - These — s
    - chemicals — s
    - smell — v
    - bad — sc
    - taste — v
    - poisonous — sc

11. She wants this job badly.
    - She — s
    - wants — v
    - job — do

12. We produce junk mail here.
    - We — s
    - produce — v
    - mail — do

13. ✍ Candidly, the systems and design engineer, Muriel Hangover, made the project even more difficult.
    - engineer — s
    - Muriel Hangover — app
    - made — v
    - project — do
    - ficult — oc

14. His big sales orders sometimes generate very tiny bonuses and gigantic headaches.
    - orders — s
    - generate — v
    - bonuses — do
    - headaches — do

15. You should never turn your unprotected back.
    - You — s
    - should — v
    - turn — v
    - back — do

16. We did not take his phone messages—his delaying tactic—Monday.
    - We — s
    - did — v
    - take — v
    - messages — do
    - tactic — app

17. Both careful and careless writers should now recognize sentence functions.
    - writers — s
    - should — v
    - recognize — v
    - functions — do

18. Her pretty gray hair, George, does not necessarily
    represent wisdom.

19. Mistakes cost the department money and anger
    clients.

20. Take a good look at your corkboard.

21. We have arranged an incredibly innovative, phe-
    nomenally creative manufacturing process.

22. Boredom, an old excuse, is no excuse.

THERAPY 3

In each of the following sentences you will find one or
more of the phrases we have discussed in this chapter: verbal phrases (participial, infinitive, or gerund), prepositional
phrases, verb phrases, absolute phrases, elliptical phrases.
The simple prepositions or verbals are italicized. Phrases
within other phrases are shown as brackets within shading.
Label each bracketed or shaded phrase. (Because you have
already practiced identifying verb phrases, we have not
bracketed those here.) When you find an elliptical phrase,
write in the missing words.

participial phrase—part   infinitive phrase—inf
gerund phrase—gerund   absolute phrase—abso
prepositional phrase—prep   elliptical phrase—ell

         prep

1. *For* a change, Marguerita Marrymenot is not
                prep
painting her nails *at her desk*.

            prep

abso   2. The mistake *behind* him, Jasper Jazenspit has
                prep   prep
been promoted *to* vice president *in* charge *of*
      prep
three-martini lunches.

         gerund   prep

3. *Coughing* loudly is cause *for* dismissal
       prep
around his office.

4. Our salespeople have difficulty *deciding*
                inf
part   whether *to phone* or *to write* potential cus-
                      prep
tomers *about* our new personally engraved
                      part
pitchforks.

                  ell

5. We know more than he [knows] *about* the
prep   part
problem *involving* his wife's phone calls.

gerund

6. *In* the meantime, we will supervise the *testing* of our products to *determine* durability and purpose.

7. An ounce *of* prevention can be much more expensive than a pound *of* cure. [is].

abso

8. Creativity *being* minimal *in* the company, I think we must have hired all left-brained people.

prep

9. He pretends *to be* deaf *at* the whisper *of* increased salaries *in* the budget.

gerund

10. *Belonging to* the health club allows one *to learn* the bare essentials.

inf

11. He's so lazy that we have *to include a self-addressed envelope to persuade* him *to mail* his insurance claims.

inf

12. *To win* an argument *with* a customer is *to lose* a sale.

13. You could die *from* rheumatoid arthritis while
    [you are] *waiting in line at the copier*.

14. The only way *to get* a vacation is *to make* a
    mistake or *to contract* typhoid

15. *Forgetting* the past, we work *toward* Friday.

THERAPY 4

In the following sentences underline the main clauses.
Put parentheses around the subordinate clauses. Label the
subordinate clauses either *adjective, adverb,* or *noun.* If
you have difficulty visualizing these clauses, review the
diagrams in Chapter 12.

1. These provisions are strictly enforced by the

   adj clause—describes *company*
   company, (which from time to time exercises its

   right to do stupid things).

2. Strafford told me the truth, but I prefer lies.

3. We want to silence our talking plants (before they

   adv clause—tells when
   give away our top secrets).

4. The blue-eyed blonde is the customer (who asked
<u>adj clause—tells which customer</u>
for a delivery date to coincide with her divorce).

adv clause—tells when
5. (As he left the 56th floor), <u>I left the building</u>.

adv clause—tells when
6. (When it is time to go to lunch), <u>wake me</u>.

noun clause—direct object of *explained*
7. <u>I explained</u> (how easily small computers fit into
briefcases).

noun clause—direct obect of *tell*
8. <u>Can you tell me</u> (why you chose a mauve-colored
lavatory)?

adv clause—tells when
9. <u>The director's nose twitches</u> (when the subject of
taxes surfaces).

10. <u>Let me explain profits to you</u>: <u>products go out</u>, and
<u>money comes in</u>. (three main clauses)

11. <u>Sue Snitt and Dwardon Blum reiterated our goals
and then sabotaged our efforts to reach them.</u>
(one clause)

12. Don't simply display the product; ask for his purchase order number.   (two main clauses)

13. noun clause—direct object of *believe*
We believe (that you share the company's concern
about rising prices and lower incentive awards).

14. noun clause—object of the
We would like to know (where you got the inside
infinitive *to know*
information).

15. adj clause—tells which code
The security code (that was cracked) is supposed to
be foolproof; what does that make you?
(two main clauses)

16. The construction cost is ridiculous (when you com-
adv clause—tells when
pare it to any other bid).

17. noun clause—direct object of *suggest*
I suggest (that you consider the possibility of your
being fired over the issue).

18. noun clause—direct object of *Tell*
Tell me (how you sold that merchandise), and
noun clause—direct object of *tell*
I'll tell you (how I figured your commission).

19. adv clause—tells when
(As soon as the doctor diagnoses Mr. Comun-

glued's psychosis), <u>the boss will tell you how to handle that customer.</u>

20. Psychotic behavior is (how he avoids the tough assignments).

noun clause—subject complement
that renames *psychotic behavior*

21. <u>The security officers looked askance at the size of my briefcase.</u>   (one main clause)

22. <u>The security officers asked</u> (why I made so many trips in and out of the building with my briefcase).

noun clause—direct object of *asked*

23. <u>The last supervisory course on avoiding sexual harassment involved role plays</u> (that required no acting at all on our part).

adj clause—describes *role plays*

24. (If the customer calls in the next few days) (before the warranty expires), <u>put him on hold.</u>

adv clause—tells when and under what condition
adv clause—tells when

25. (That the deadline is Friday) <u>doesn't seem to bother him.</u>

noun clause—subject of *doesn't seem*

THERAPY 5

Identify clauses and sentence patterns in the following sentences. Circle the simple subjects and simple predicates (verbs) of each clause. Underline main clauses, and place parentheses around subordinate clauses. Use brackets to show subordinate clauses inside subordinate clauses. In the margin label the sentence patterns: simple, compound, complex, or compound-complex.

complex

1. (If (you) (like) these notepads [that (I) (ordered)]), (I) (will plan) to write you more notes on motivational mannerisms.

simple

2. (You) (may have) to tie him with his own red tape to get him in the sales meeting.

complex

3. (If the (lawsuit) (fits)), (you) (settle) out of court.

complex

4. (What the (world) (needs) now) , (is) a good $20 steak.

compound-complex

5. This consultant's (project) (is) an ongoing process; (it) (will) not (end) (until all our (budget) (has been exhausted)).

complex
6. (Where we have given generous bonuses), we have also harnessed much brainpower.

simple
7. Riding a horse to work saves gas and clears the freeways of traffic.

simple
8. All our new employees attend an orientation session to learn to pronounce the boss's name.

complex
9. Seniority around our office means (that you have much patience and no backbone).

compound-complex
10. I wouldn't say (that the meeting was a long one), but we sent out our laundry.

complex
11. It would appear (that no one is in charge here).

complex
12. ((Whoever laughs last) is assigned) the project.

complex   13. ((Whoever has all the answers)) evidently does not understand all the questions.

compound-complex   14. Attached is the schedule showing (what time you reported to work each morning last year); therefore, we trust (that you have recorded the correct hours on your records also).

complex   15. We have examined our files and have determined (that you are currently exempt from receiving a paycheck).

complex   16. (Although I agree [that your plan is an excellent idea]), the system needs some refining.

compound   17. We entered the product name for each new account, the customer number for each old account, the invoicing procedure for each division, the contact name and address for each order; thus, the report is consistent and brief.

compound

18. We have emergency plans for all kinds of inclement weather such as hurricanes, tornadoes, hailstorms, and nuclear fallout; there are no provisions for rain.

simple

19. The trustees asked the committee to meet during the first quarter because of the confusion and cost of two separate billings, the decision of some residents not to subscribe to the service, and the desire to be more specific about the expenses of the maintenance fund.

complex

20. I asked Lawrence L. Lamkin to set up an appointment with his supervisor and me (so that we could make some determination about his future with the company).

compound-complex

21. I asked Sara Hooper (if it were true [that she had been estimating the figures in our reports]), and she stated (that in a few instances [when things did not add up] she had altered the numbers).

complex

22. Your representative has been briefed on these procedures and will be able to answer any question you may have, (as long as they are limited to price and availability)

compound-complex

23. All our retailers and distributors want motor-oil products (that can be promoted at the price shown in the three ads running in today's paper), and (as you know), this plan is not feasible (because most of the sales people do not see the ads of their products).

compound-complex

24. We are unaware of any reason to withdraw the product from the market; but (if you feel [that you want a product] [that you works]), please let us know, and we will attempt to correct the difficulties.

complex

25. Did you really expect this machine to work (when you ordered it)?

simple
26. (you) Please instruct your officers to review the credit files for current financial information, to provide all necessary information for the loan application, and to delineate the strength of your credit position.

complex
27. (Unless you plan to appear before the board after an extended fast), your efficiency in making the presentation has little to do with management's acceptance of the idea (that the company cafeteria should be subsidized).

complex
28. Before leaving on vacation, (you) please check with the personnel office to see (if you will have a job [when you return]).

complex
29. We think (that your attendance at this meeting is a necessity), (no matter how boring it is).

complex
30. (That he frowns [when he hears the boss's name]) must mean (that he has some rec-

ollection of his life before the head injury).

simple

31. With the conclusion of this chapter, (you)
(know) enough grammar terms to pass the
state board exam for speakers of English.

THERAPY 8

Correct the pronoun errors in the following sentences.
Explain your answers by identifying how the pronoun
functions in each sentence (subject, appositive of a subject,
subject complement, direct object, indirect object, object
of a preposition, object of an infinitive, appositive of an
object, subject of an infinitive). Remember this tip: Omit
the other people named in the sentence and then trust your
ear for the correct pronoun choice.

1. I have been advised by Sam Sledgehammer, Jody
   him
   Jaggernut and he about the situation developing
   with the basement flooding. (obj of
   preposition *by*)

2. Tutty Taylor, Tarzan Tamerick, and myself all
   brought the matter to his attention. (subject)

3. Tell ~~whomever~~ *whoever* answers the phone that the boss is in conference and cannot take the call. (subject of *answers*)

4. Your marketing representative can arrange for Marge Gluttenheimer or ~~I~~ *me* to contact you before Friday for last-minute details.
(obj. of preposition *for* and subject of the infinitive *to contact*)

5. Our president, Helen Garter, has reviewed your resume, along with those of students from several other universities. As a result, ~~her~~ *she* and I have selected several candidates for further interviews; you are not one of them. (subject)

6. If you have any questions, please don't ask Joanne, Bubba, Binky, or ~~I~~ *me* for answers. (direct object)

7. The attorney explained all the details of the settlement to ~~whomever~~ *whoever* called his office on Friday.
(subject of the verb *called*)

8. Address this complaint about the purple carpet to ~~who~~ *whom*? (obj. of prep. *to*)

9. The supervisors, ~~us~~ _we_ in this office included, have

   already kissed all the babies we intend to kiss.
   (In apposition to the subject *supervisors*)

10. My manager, ~~who~~ _whom_ I consider antagonistic, holds

    the purse strings to my future dress-for-success

    look. (direct object of *I consider—I consider whom [him]
    antagonistic.*)

11. The operation involves several department heads

    from Dallas—Tom Jones, Mike Sparks, and ~~I~~ _me_—as

    well as those from Atlanta. (In apposition with the direct
    object *department heads*)

12. I fired him, although he is a person ~~who~~ _whom_ I respect.
    (direct object of the verb *respect*)

13. By phoning the support center or ~~myself~~ _me_ personally,

    you can get any information you need.
    (object of the gerund *phoning*)

14. Let me know if John or ~~him~~ _he_ can conduct the inter-

    views for belly dancers.
    (subject of *can conduct*)

15. He asked that they write Wade Johnson or ~~I~~ _me_ about

    the agreement. (direct object of the verb *write*)

THERAPY 7

Correct the subject-verb agreement errors in the following sentences. Write "correct" in the margin beside the statements without errors. Underline all simple subjects and verbs.

1. The number of attachments included with these forms is exceeded only by the number of attachments enclosed with the last form we sent you.

2. The array of educational programs benefits both the student and the company.

3. Inside this old file cabinet is a collector's item commonly known as the pencil.

4. The deficiency in math and science skills among the top executives points to major problems of productivity.

Correct

5. Want ads say that all job categories from

receptionist to undertaker require a high
level of mathematical skills.

6. Shuffling added, amended, qualified, and
initialed paragraphs certainly make a contract look negotiable. (One action)

7. We have been told that the equipment at all
branches need repairs.

Correct 8. Three hours is a long time to be in the air,
particularly without a parachute. (*Three
hours* represents a single unit of time.)

9. Neither lack of money nor lack of praise
keep John from coming to the office each
day. (Subjects linked by neither/nor are
treated as separate elements. Both are singular here.)

10. He outlined all the errors in our reasoning
that has caused us continuing problems. (If
that refers to *reasoning*, the sentence is

correct as written. Here verb choice dictates meaning!)

11. Each <u>manager</u>, along with all the sales peo-
ple in the territory, ~~are~~ ^{is} eligible to attend the seminar.

12. In defense of everything I said yesterday during the meeting ~~is~~ ^{are} the signed <u>contracts</u>.

13. We have not <u>talked</u> with a <u>single one</u> of the instructors who ~~have~~ ^{has} <u>complained</u> about having you in our seminar. (This sentence means no instructor they talked to has complained. But the sentence can be correct as written; *who* can refer to *instructors*. In that case, the sentence means that they have not talked with any of the complaining instructors. Again, verb choice dictates sentence meaning!)

14. <u>All</u> of the painting including the other maintenance work ~~have~~ ^{has} been completed.

15. He has a file containing several of our com-
    <u>plaints</u>, which <u>need</u>ˢ daily updating. (If
    which refers to *complaints* [highly unlikely
    here], the sentence is correct as written.
    Here again, verb choice dictates meaning.)

Correct   16. My <u>interest</u> is primarily stocks and bonds.

THERAPY 8

Correct the unnecessary viewpoint, voice, mood, or tense changes in the following sentences.

1. I am planning a retirement luncheon for Taylor
   Toyauski, and I ~~would~~ recommend that the luncheon ~~is~~ be held before he ~~left~~ leaves the company.

2. We have confirmed reservations in your name, ~~and~~
   ~~your room charges~~ we have ~~been~~ prepaid ~~by us also~~.
   your room charges also.
   (Also correct: *Reservations in your name have been
   confirmed.* . . .)

3. We have compiled *Manpower and the Monkey* to
   give you the necessary information, and ~~it was~~ we have

edited and updated~~it~~as we have experienced a quantum leap of energy.

4. Managers should comment on writing skills in performance appraisals, and ~~you~~they should also recommend self-study texts for improvements. (Also correct: *You should comment . . .*)

5. All of the expenses that go on the forms for reimbursement should be approved by department heads or their designated representatives. ~~Please~~The approver should review these for accuracy. (Who is to review these? The viewpoint change makes the "doer" in the second sentence unclear. Also correct: *You should have all of the expenses that go on the forms for reimbursement approved by . . . Please review these . . .*)

6. This system makes it easy for you to boost payments on long-standing accounts. ~~Users~~You will also have an invaluable checklist of ten ways to spot a company in financial trouble. (Are these sentences talking about two different groups of people? You and other users? Also correct: *This system will*

make it easy for users to boost payments on long-standing accounts. Users will also . . .)

7. This situation seems to have slipped out of hand, and I ~~would~~ suggest that we call in a consultant immediately to see if we can dismiss the whole crew and start over.

8. The instructor must provide a recommended reading list by August; the ^(student must pay) tuition ~~will be paid~~ in full by September. (Will the instructor pay the tuition also? The switch to passive voice makes the sentence unclear. Also correct: *A recommended reading list will be provided . . .)*

9. Please sign here, and ~~you should~~ also pay me now. (Also correct: *You should sign here . . .)*

10. The managers gathered at his retirement dinner, and ^(expressed) great eagerness to say goodbye ~~was expressed~~.

THERAPY 9

Punctuate the following sentences.

1. Before talking to his sales team each morning, the boss takes two aspirin and a vodka. (Comma to set off introductory verbal phrase)

2. The company's primary product, Jemitone, is currently marketed under various trade names. (Commas to enclose an appositive)

3. Our products are marketed for use in Europe, a limited market; Latin America, one of our leading markets; Asia; Africa; and Australia. (Separate the items in the series with semicolons because some of the items already have internal commas.)

4. Granted, we do want to emphasize that the fight has just begun. (Comma to set off introductory word)

5. A five-year search involving six companies across the United States has proven unsuccessful according to the results. (Be careful here not to simply separate subject and verb with a comma. Also correct: *A five-year search, involving six companies across the United Sates, has* . . . Commas to set off these two phrases subordinate a nonessential idea.)

6. Our company has a sound balance sheet with no need of near-term financing, but the current ratio at the end of the third quarter of this fiscal year was not what we expected. (Comma to separate independent clauses)

7. Other leukocytes are natural killer lymphocytes that kill virus-infected cells; scavenger cells amplify immune effects. (Semicolon to separate independent clauses when a conjunction is missing)

8. Although we have seen little movement so far, the predicted stock market gains are possible. (Comma to set off introductory clause)

9. Because I do not have a crystal ball, I cannot predict whether future products will have the same consequences on our sales; therefore, we are giving you a flat salary despite your efforts in selling. (Comma to set off introductory clause; semicolon to separate independent clauses; comma after *therefore* to set off introductory, transition word) (Also correct: Insert a period rather than a semicolon before *therefore*.)

10. The seminar presents a practical, indulgent philosophy toward those who work in our company. (Comma to separate two adjectives equally modifying a noun; no comma before the *who* clause because it is essential)

11. He wanted to know whether to produce the product or to pull the ads from TV. (No question mark here. The sentence contains an *indirect* question, not a direct question.)

12. This is the last report I intend to write; it includes everything I know on the subjects of finance and manufacturing. (Semicolon to separate independent clause when conjunction is missing) (Also correct: Insert a period rather than a semicolon before *it*.)

13. These packages were shipped Tuesday, July 6, to Atlanta, Georgia, for use in their computer literacy courses, accounting courses, and typing courses. (Commas to enclose date and state; commas to separate items in a series) (Also correct: You may omit the comma after *Georgia* and the final comma in the series.)

14. Our building is so cold that they issue wool underwear with the uniforms. (No commas to set off the essential *that* clause)

15. His tardiness record needs improvement; in fact, we've taken out the time clock and installed a calendar. (Semicolon to separate independent clauses

when conjunction is missing; comma to set off introductory phrase to last clause) (Also correct: Insert a period rather than a semicolon after *improvement*.)

16. In their annual reports prepared by my organization, we translate "big losses" to "unrealized gains." (Comma to set off long introductory phrases; period inside quotation marks regardless of meaning)

17. Eulonda should know, if at all possible, about our lack of progress in gaining support for our incentive-award idea, a trip to the Orient. (Commas to enclose interrupting phrase; comma to set off an appositive) (Also correct: Insert a dash or colon instead of a comma after *idea*.)

18. To ensure stability at each branch site in Alaska, please make sure the job matches the applicant. (Comma to set off introductory verbal phrase)

19. Jody cannot understand the promotion policies around here and, to be sure his efforts do not go

unnoticed, asks for a performance review after each
sale. (Commas to enclose a nonessential interrupting
clause coming between the compound verbs *cannot
understand* and *asks*)

20. If the research results are unfavorable, you had bet-
    ter have enough paperwork to show for the effort.
    (Comma to set off introductory clause)

21. We're on a time-management program: the boss
    manages to see that we have time. (The last inde-
    pendent clause further explains the first clause.)
    (Also correct: Insert a dash rather than a colon after
    program.)

22. He has a great deal of authority with his job, but at
    home he has control only of whether he drinks tea
    or coffee, where he dumps his garbage, and when he
    breathes. (Comma before a coordinate conjunction
    to separate independent clauses; the remaining
    commas to separate a series of clauses) (Also cor-
    rect: Omit the final comma in the series.)

23. In the first report in the subsection entitled "Pricing," we have included all the guidelines you need. (Comma to set off long introductory prepositional phrases; comma inside quotation marks regardless of meaning)

24. I cannot identify the source of the expense-reimbursement memo, which I think is the most confusing memo ever to arrive on my desk. (Comma to set off nonessential *which* clause)

25. He's the kind of employee who can find a cloud overhanging every silver lining. (No comma to set off the essential *who* clause)

26. I mailed the book Tuesday morning, although it may not have had proper postage. (Comma to set off a nonessential afterthought)

27. He asked me if I knew there would be a price increase June 1. (No question mark after an indirect question)

28. He asked me, "Do you know if there will be a price

    increase June 1?" (Quotation marks to enclose a di-

    rect quote; question mark after direct question in-

    side the quotation marks)

29. Punctuation dictates meaning, doesn't it? (Comma

    to set off a tagged-on afterthought or question)

THERAPY 10

See if you can spot the errors (capitalization, hyphenation, apostrophes, misused words) in the following sentences.

1. Our Company demands confidentiality in these di-

    rect mail campaigns.

2. He has never received a promotion since working
    there
    their; he attributes his lack of success to the fact

    that he was born on Friday, February 13.

3. He does not seem to understand the problem well

    enough to present any solution.

4. The manager has outlined a step-by-step approach for failure.

5. I think you can say our company is over regulated. We have sixty-six Policies for operating the elevators safely.

6. The doors in our office building, too, do not yet have signs; its difficult, therefore, too distinguish restrooms from storage closets.

7. He says that may be the plan will work and may be it won't. (Adverbs meaning *possibly*)

8. The three supervisors status reports reflect they're *their* attitudes about the problem approach.

9. Mr. Johnson ensures *assures* us that we will get their business.

10. Donald Blumberhead is a Manager who's *whose* experience qualifies him only to empty the garbage.

THERAPY 11

Identify and correct things in the following sentences that may raise eyebrows—questionable or incorrect constructions.

1. You have to be computer literate to ~~really~~ foul things up. (Split infinitive and prepositional ending. The prepositional ending can be appropriate here because this sentence is informal. The split infinitive may add emphasis.) Another alternative: *You have to be computer literate really to foul up things.*)

2. We haven~~'t~~ never said that this product was no good. (Double negative in the first clause) (Also correct: *We haven't ever . . .*)

3. He made an issue of pointing out all the mistakes, which should not have upset the writer. (Did the mistakes upset the writer, or did pointing out the mistakes upset the writer? Rewrite: . . . *mistakes. His efforts should not have . . .* Or: . . . *mistakes. The mistakes, however, should not have . . .*)

4. The telegrams he sends always get results. How-
   ever, they may be expensive. Unclear reference.
       ~~?~~
   What is expensive—the results or the telegrams?
   Rewrite: . . . *However, the results may* . . . Or: . . .
   However, the telegrams may . . .)

5. The director has assigned me to correct the problem,
   which my boss sees as an advantage. (Unclear refer-
     ~~?~~
   ence. Does *which* refer to the problem or the whole
   idea? Rewrite: *The director has assigned me to cor-*
   rect the problem, and my boss sees my being as-
   signed to the project as an advantage. Or: *The*
   director has assigned me to correct the problem;
   however, my boss sees the problem as an advan-
   tage.)

6. He suggested more water coolers and ~~that we give~~
   ~~employees~~ shorter work periods between breaks.
   (Unparallel construction. Another possible rewrite:
   He suggested that we install more water coolers
   and that we give . . .)

7. Please take a moment to (thoroughly) read this chapter in case your next boss is a former English teacher. (Split infinitive)

8. Let me know if I can help you, and the results. *let me know* (Unparallel construction)

9. You should have picked up the application blank *that* ~~which~~ allows you to enter the sales contest. (Ambiguous use of *which* for *that*.)

10. I want to (ultimately) verify all such claims of sanity. (Split infinitive)

11. We can always hope for an increase in salary and to ~~get~~ a longer vacation. (Unparallel construction— *for* Another possible rewrite: *We can always hope to get a salary increase or to get more vacation.*)

12. Sparky Skymouth is the employee ~~which~~ I hired the *whom or that*

morning of my hangover. (Relative pronoun error. *Which* can't refer to people.)

13. The slump in sales has resulted in our getting the new advertising contract; that[?] is something we need to discuss in our Friday meeting. (Unclear pronoun reference. Does *that* refer to the contract or to the sales slump? Rewrite: *. . . contract; this sales slump . . .* Or: *. . . contract; this contract is . . .*)

14. I did not see ~~neither~~ *either* the letter or the resume. (Double negative. Another possible rewrite: *I saw neither the letter nor the resume.*)

15. The blueprints do not refer to the DPX number, the invoice number, or ~~what number is on~~ the order *number*. (Unparallel construction)

16. While *I was* away at the conference, my desk was moved into the hallway. (Dangler—the desk wasn't away. Another possible rewrite: *While I was away at the*

*conference, someone moved my desk into the hall-
way.*)

17. He suggested revising the rules of the sales campaign or ~~that we could~~ eliminate^ing employee participation. (Unparallel construction. Another possible
rewrite: *He suggested that we could revise the rules
of the sales campaign or eliminate . . .*)

18. After forcing my opinion down his throat,\ ^I postponed the dis-
cussion~~was postponed~~. (Dangler—the discussion
didn't force the opinion. Another possible rewrite:
*After I forced my opinion down his throat, I post-
poned the discussion.*)

19. ^He realized that I could not handle the problem,~~which he realized~~?
(Unclear reference. Did he realize the problem or
realize that the writer could not handle the problem? Another possible rewrite: *I could not handle
the problem, a fact he realized.* Or: *I could not
handle the problem, and he realized that fact.*)

20. These reports are clearer than last month's reports (Unclear comparison)

21. Your questions are outside of my area of expertise. (Unnecessary preposition)

INDEX

241

ABOUT THE AUTHOR

Dianna Booher is president of Houston-based Booher Writing Consultants, among whose clients are many FORTUNE 500 corporations, including IBM, Exxon, and Tenneco. This is her 19th book. Some of her most recent titles are WOULD YOU PUT THAT IN WRITING?, SEND ME A MEMO, THE NEW SECRETARY, and CUTTING PAPERWORK IN THE CORPORATE CULTURE.